PRAISE FOR
FROM SECRET BALLOT TO DEMOCRACY SAUSAGE

'This book unravels mysteries, and explains the quirks and triumphs of Australia. It answers questions you didn't even know you had. I learned something on every page.'
WALEED ALY

'Australia led the world in broadening the franchise and introducing the secret ballot, but few nations followed us down the path of compulsory voting. This absorbing book explains a century-old institution, how it came to be, and how it survives.'
ANTONY GREEN

'The Australian way of voting seems—to us—entirely ordinary but, as Judith Brett reveals, it's a singular miracle of innovation of which we can all be fiercely proud. This riveting and deeply researched little book is full of jaw-dropping moments. Like the time that South Australian women accidentally won the right to stand as candidates—an international first. Or the horrifying debates that preceded the Australian parliament's shameful decision to disenfranchise Aborigines in 1902. This is the story of a young democracy that is unique. A thrilling and valuable book.'
ANNABEL CRABB

Judith Brett is the author of *Robert Menzies' Forgotten People* and emeritus professor of politics at La Trobe University in Melbourne. *The Enigmatic Mr Deakin* won the 2018 National Biography Award, and was shortlisted in the Prime Minister's Literary Awards, NSW Premier's Literary Awards, NSW Premier's History Awards and Queensland Literary Awards.

FROM SECRET BALLOT
TO DEMOCRACY SAUSAGE

HOW AUSTRALIA GOT COMPULSORY VOTING

JUDITH BRETT

t

TEXT PUBLISHING MELBOURNE AUSTRALIA

textpublishing.com.au

The Text Publishing Company
Swann House
22 William Street
Melbourne Victoria 3000
Australia

Copyright © Judith Brett, 2019

The moral right of Judith Brett to be identified as the author of this work has been asserted.

All rights reserved. Without limiting the rights under copyright above, no part of this publication shall be reproduced, stored in or introduced into a retrieval system, or transmitted in any form or by any means (electronic, mechanical, photocopying, recording or otherwise), without the prior permission of both the copyright owner and the publisher of this book.

Published by The Text Publishing Company, 2019

Cover design by W. H. Chong
Page design by Text
Typeset by J&M Typesetting

Printed and bound in Australia by Griffin Press, an accredited ISO/NZS 14001:2004 Environmental Management System printer

ISBN: 9781925603842 (paperback)
ISBN: 9781925626810 (ebook)

A catalogue record for this book is available from the National Library of Australia.

This book is printed on paper certified against the Forest Stewardship Council® Standards. Griffin Press holds FSC chain-of-custody certification SGS-COC-005088. FSC promotes environmentally responsible, socially beneficial and economically viable management of the world's forests.

CONTENTS

1.	Our Majoritarian Democracy	1
2.	The Invention of the Australian Ballot	11
3.	Three South Australian Innovators	27
4.	Directly Chosen by the People	45
5.	Women In, Aborigines Out	53
6.	Administering Elections Impartially	73
7.	Counting the Vote	85
8.	Early Arguments over Compulsory Voting	93
9.	Labor in Power	101
10.	Voting on Saturday	111
11.	Queensland Makes It Compulsory	117
12.	The Farmers Get a Party	125
13.	Compulsory Voting Achieved	131
14.	The Rise of Minor Parties and the Senate	139
15.	Liberals Push Back	145
16.	Australian Election Days	155
17.	Of Plebiscites and Surveys	165
18.	We Are Good at Elections	175
	Acknowledgments	184
	Notes	185
	Bibliography	195
	List of Illustrations	199

1

OUR MAJORITARIAN DEMOCRACY

NOT MANY COUNTRIES compel their citizens to vote, but Australia is one. Voting is compulsory in nineteen of the world's 166 electoral democracies and only nine strictly enforce it.[1] None of Europe's most influential democracies has it, and none of the countries in the mainstream of Australia's political development: not the United Kingdom, the United States, Canada, New Zealand or Ireland.

People from our sister democracies are often astonished that Australians are compelled to turn up to vote: it seems an affront to freedom. We in reply are appalled at their low turnouts and the election of leaders and governments by a minority of voters. In the 2016 American presidential election the percentage turnout was in the high fifties. Donald Trump did not have the support of the majority of voters, but neither would Hillary Clinton had she won.[2] Britain's disastrous 2016 decision to leave the European Union was carried by a slim majority of the 72.2 per cent of voters who turned out.[3] At Canada's 2015 election, which brought Justin Trudeau to power, the turnout of 68.3 per cent was the highest in twenty years.[4] These are percentages of registered voters, not of all those eligible to vote. In none of these countries is it compulsory to be on the electoral roll. In Australia registration has been compulsory since 1911. Turnout in Australian elections is always above 90 per cent of registered voters, and in the high eighties of those eligible to enrol.[5]

It has been compulsory to vote in Australian federal elections since 1924, when a private member's bill passed through both houses in a single day with scarcely any debate. Geoffrey Sawer, doyen of Australia's legal historians, famously wrote, 'No major departure in the federal political system had ever been made in so casual a fashion.'[6] Sawer was wrong: the ease of the bill's passage was not because of lack of attention. Rather, it was uncontroversial because it expressed the political culture that had developed in Australia since the middle of the nineteenth century, when the colonies became self-governing.

This political culture was majoritarian and bureaucratic. Australians wanted their governments to have the support of the majority of electors, they preferred their elections to be orderly and they were happy for them to be run by government officials. By the time voting was made compulsory for federal elections, the arguments for and against had been thoroughly aired, and for thirteen years it had been compulsory for all eligible adults to be on the electoral roll. The paucity of debate Sawer noted was not a sign of indifference but of relaxed acceptance of an outcome long in the making.

Support for compulsory voting among Australians is consistently high. Since the earliest opinion polls on the matter, in 1943, it has never been less than 60 per cent. Support grew in the decades following World War Two and since 1967 it has bounced around in the 70-per-cent range. The lowest was 64 per cent in 1987, and the highest 77 per cent in 1969 and 2007, both elections in which there was a surge to Labor. Respondents were also asked if they would vote if it were voluntary and more than 80 per cent said Yes.[7] They were telling the truth. This is around the number who took part in the non-compulsory same-sex marriage survey in 2017. When it was first introduced, the penalty for not voting was high: two pounds, or $160 in today's money.[8] In 2017 the fine for not voting in a federal election without adequate reason was only $20, scarcely enough to compel a high turnout. It is also permissible simply to turn up to the polling booth, have one's name crossed off and leave the ballot paper blank, though surprisingly few take this option. Most invalid votes are the results of confusion.[9]

How did compulsory voting become so entrenched in Australia's political culture and why is it that, alone among English-speaking democracies, Australia compels its citizens to vote? Who pushed for voting to be made compulsory, in what circumstances and using which arguments? Who argued against it? How, and why, did these arguments fail? What other aspects of our electoral system support the acceptance of compulsory voting?

Compulsory voting and enrolment are not the only distinctive features of our elections. We vote on Saturdays, the United Kingdom on Thursdays because it was once market day, and the United States on Tuesdays. We have preferential voting, whereas the norm is first-past-the-post, in which the candidate with the most votes wins. We can vote at any electoral booth in our home state, as well as interstate and at our overseas embassies and consulates. And our elections are run by government bureaucrats, according to uniform rules, with political parties and politicians at arm's-length.

Australia's embrace of compulsory voting tells us a great deal about the way our history has shaped our political culture. When he was president, Barack Obama praised Australia's mandatory voting and said that if everybody in the United States voted, 'it would completely change the political map in this country because the people who tend not to vote are young. They are lower-income. They are skewed more heavily towards immigrant groups and minority groups.' Mandatory voting would counteract the power of money in determining elections, he said, and encourage lawmakers to make it easier rather than harder for people to vote. Obama stopped short, however, of calling for a change in the law.[10] No doubt he knew that this would have little chance in a country which places a higher value on the liberty of the individual than on the collective good. Too many would argue that it was undemocratic, authoritarian, an infringement of an individual's rights.

The United States and Australia were both settled by people from the British Isles, who brought with them the political traditions and ideas of their home country, but they were settled in different centuries. The dominant political ideas were different, and so were the problems which preoccupied political reformers and which they tried to solve in these two new societies.

Liberal democracies are hybrid political systems which combine the rule of law and commitment to civil rights with popular elections and majority rule. There are obvious tensions between the need to protect individuals from the tyranny of the majority and the need for the majority to be protected from powerful minority vested interests. Australians are as appalled by American gun laws, with their protection of the right of individuals to bear arms, as Americans are by our compulsory voting—more so, as compulsory voting never killed anyone. Different polities strike different balances. Where the United States favours liberty and rights over democracy and majorities, we favour democracy and majorities over liberty and rights.

The early settlers to America left Britain when parliament was still struggling to wrest control of government from the monarch and when individuals were persecuted for their religious beliefs. America's informing spirit is the seventeenth-century English philosopher John Locke. In his *Two Treatises of Government* Locke rejected the divine right of kings and argued that a government's authority derived from a social contract among individuals who transferred some of their natural rights to life, liberty and property to a government. If the government failed to protect these rights, then these rights-bearing individuals could legitimately overthrow it. Locke was a Puritan, and his argument justified parliament's revolt against the two Stuart kings Charles I and James II.

Locke gave the Americans the arguments they used to declare their independence from the distant autocratic British government and establish a new nation. The Declaration of Independence begins:

> We hold these truths to be self-evident, that all men are created equal, that they are endowed by their Creator with certain unalienable Rights, that among these are Life, Liberty and the pursuit of Happiness.—That to secure these rights, Governments are instituted among Men, deriving their just powers from the consent of the governed,—That whenever any Form of Government becomes destructive of these ends, it is the Right of the People to alter or to abolish it, and to institute new Government.

The important point to notice here is that individuals and their rights come first, and that government comes after. It is a bottom-up movement in which the state only has as much authority as is transferred to it by its citizens for purposes of mutual benefit and protection. This makes compulsory voting a logical impossibility. If it is the votes of free, rights-bearing citizens which create the state and give legitimacy to its authority, then the state cannot compel citizens to vote as it has not yet been voted into existence.

I am using the term 'state' to refer to the collection of official institutions which wield legitimate authority over the residents of a particular territory: the parliament or lawmaking institutions, the executive that carries out the law and the judiciary that enforces it. The term 'government' is often loosely used for the same purpose, but it also has a narrower meaning referring only to the executive branch of the state.

By the time the Australian colonies were establishing their political institutions, in the late eighteenth and nineteenth centuries, the British parliament had well and truly defeated the autocratic monarchs. Britain was a constitutional monarchy, with legislative and executive power firmly in the hands of the parliament and the monarch reduced to a largely ceremonial role. The franchise was expanding, and the British government, not wanting to lose its Australian colonies as it had its American, ruled them with a light touch. When the colonies started politely to request self-government, it was granted. Where John Locke was the foundational thinker for the United States, for Australia it was the philosopher and political reformer Jeremy Bentham, who was writing in the late eighteenth and early nineteenth centuries as Australia was being settled.[11]

Bentham rejected the idea of natural or divinely given rights which precede the establishment of government. He argued instead that rights are created by law; that without government and law there are no rights. Government first, then rights. He also believed that government should be guided by what he called the principle of utility: that government policies and actions should advance the greatest happiness for the greatest number, with each person counting as one. British government in the early nineteenth century was patently not doing this. Power was in the hands of a small landed elite, who governed for the interests of their class while the lives of many were blighted by want and misery. Bentham wrote lengthy accounts of schemes for the reform of Britain's political and legal institutions, including for manhood suffrage (the right for all men to vote regardless of property or income) and the secret ballot. He attracted many followers, including James Mill and his son John Stuart Mill, who developed his ideas and popularised them among people interested in political reform.[12]

Bentham held a much more expansive view of the possibilities of government action than did America's founding fathers, with their elaborate checks and balances, and this suited the circumstances of the Australian colonies. New colonies demand 'ample government', wrote Edward Gibbon Wakefield, whose ideas on systematic colonisation inspired the establishment of South Australia. Australia's colonies needed roads, bridges, ports, railways and irrigation works, and later gas, electricity, sewerage and the telegraph—in short, all the infrastructure required for a modern exporting economy—and it was provided by the government. The historian W. K. Hancock famously summed this up:

> The Australian democracy has come to look upon the State as a vast public utility, whose duty is to provide the greatest happiness for the greatest number… To the Australian the State means collective power at the service of individualistic 'rights' and therefore he sees no opposition between his individualism and his reliance on governments.[13]

What's more, for the first hundred years or so Australian taxpayers didn't even have to pay much for the services government provided. The threat of taxation, a major motivator of liberalism's defence of individual rights and arguments for small government, was largely missing. The British government paid for the early Australian governments. Remembering the American colonies' revolt over taxation without representation, it decided not to tax the Australian settlers. Britain would gain its economic return instead from increased trade and investment opportunities. Nor did Australia have to pay for its own defence, as this too was provided by the British government. With little taxation, why would people want to limit government expenditure on services that benefited them? 'So,' writes the historian John Hirst, 'the function of government changed in Australia: it was not primarily to keep order within and defeat enemies without; it was a resource which settlers could draw on to make money.'[14] The paternalism of the Australian state is based on the circumstances of our settlement.

Even after self-government was granted and the Australian colonies had to pay their way, individual Australians remained free of direct taxation. Governments raised taxes through land sales and duties on imports, and they built infrastructure largely on borrowed money. Incomes remained untaxed until the late nineteenth and early twentieth centuries. The federal government did not tax income until 1915, when it needed to raise money to fight the Great War. By then settler Australians' view of government as a major source of benefit rather than a circumscriber of freedom was entrenched. Government came before society in Australia and was gratefully accepted. Social-contract theory, which was developed to justify the overthrow of oppressive governments, never got off the ground.

In the second half of the nineteenth and early twentieth centuries, Australia led the world in electoral reform. 'No modern democracy,' writes the American political scientist Louise Overacker, 'has shown greater readiness to experiment with various electoral methods than Australia.'[15] It was a laboratory for new ideas about democracy, and new methods of achieving them. Property qualifications were all but gone for men for lower-house elections in the populous south-eastern colonies by the end of the 1850s. Colonial politicians had invented the ballot paper and the compartmentalised polling booth to ensure secret voting, and the Australian ballot, as it became known, quickly spread around the world. In 1894 South Australian women won the right to vote, a year after women in New Zealand, along with the right to stand for parliament, which was a world-first. South Australia also established the first non-partisan, government-run electoral office to manage elections.

Two of our innovations, though, have found few followers: compulsory voting and our rejection of first-past-the-post in favour of preferential voting. Few countries use preferential voting, and then only for some elections. We use it for them all.[16] Preferential voting is as distinctively Australian as compulsory voting. Both ensure that the governments we elect have the support of the majority of voters.

At the end of the nineteenth century, after the colonial politicians had hammered out a constitution for a new, federated nation, men (and women in South and Western Australia) voted on whether to accept it. The question was simple: 'Are you in favour of the proposed Federal Constitutional Bill? Yes or No.' In 1898 the answer was No, but, after some amendments, at a second referendum a year later it was Yes and the new Commonwealth was proclaimed on New Year's Day, 1901.

The elections for the first federal parliament were run according to the laws of the states; once elected, the new parliament had to settle on how future federal elections would be run and who would be eligible to vote. The federal Franchise Act and the federal Electoral Act were both passed in 1902, the first quickly, the second after extensive debate. The disenfranchisement of Australia's indigenous people, even as white women were being given the vote, is notorious, but in most other ways these two acts were astonishingly democratic and they laid the foundations of our electoral system. There were crucial developments in 1911, when Labor made registration compulsory and introduced Saturday voting; in 1918, when preferential voting came in; and in 1924, when voting too was made compulsory.

Australia was born not on the battlefield but at the ballot box. Sixteen years after the 1899 referendum which accepted the constitution, and fourteen after the Commonwealth was proclaimed in 1901, the nation was born again, on the Gallipoli Peninsula, as the mettle of its men was tested by war. The Anzac Legend is a core Australian foundation myth. But we need more than stories of blood and heroic sacrifice, compelling as these will always be, if we are to understand our peacetime nation. The story of how we got compulsory voting is no less definitive of who we are.

Electoral history is detailed, and it can seem an arcane and specialist area, but the angels of our democracy are in this detail. Its heroes are bureaucrats and parliamentarians, not soldiers and explorers—but they too made our nation. The political stability we have enjoyed for more than a century is evidence of the care they took to create democratic, flexible electoral practices.

2

THE INVENTION OF THE AUSTRALIAN BALLOT

THE FIRST PARLIAMENTARY election on the Australian continent was held more than fifty years after Britain established the penal colony at Port Jackson, now Sydney. Self-government was not for convicts, so the tentative beginnings of the representative institutions befitting a free society had to wait until after 1840, when transportation to the east coast was all but abolished. In 1843 elections were held for twenty-four members of the thirty-six-member Legislative Council of New South Wales. The Council had existed since 1823, when five members were appointed to advise the colony's governor. Its numbers had expanded in the interim, and now two-thirds were to be elected. The remaining twelve were appointed by the governor and the Council's powers were still limited to advising. For the election, the colony was divided into twenty-four districts, including Port Phillip (now Victoria), which was then part of New South Wales.

These first elections were run according to British practice.

Nominations were made in public, generally outside pubs, which provided ready supplies of refreshments at the expense of the competing candidates, including to the many voteless men who came along to watch. This was called 'treating', and there was also bribery, both outright and disguised, such as paying for empty tasks. Only about one in five men could vote, but anyone could come along to hear the speeches. Bands played and rival groups of supporters in their candidates' colours gathered round the rostrum to cheer and boo, their enthusiasm encouraged by the free drink.

The crowds were there again on voting day. Voting too was public, again most often at the pub, with more refreshments on hand. Electors wrote the name of their preferred candidate on a piece of paper, signed it and handed it to the returning officer, who also asked them to say out loud for whom they had voted. This allowed those paying for the treating to know if their investment had paid off. A running tally was posted every hour and in close votes passions ran high as drunken electors were steered to the returning officer's desk and candidates' agents rode out to round up stragglers.[1]

Rowdy crowds of voters and onlookers enjoyed the carnival atmosphere and the candidates' largesse. Entertainment was provided even when a seat was uncontested. In 1843 on nomination day in Goulburn the sole candidate, William Bradley, provided class-nuanced festivities: roasted bullock and four barrels of ale in the town's marketplace for the humbler inhabitants, fine dining at a local inn for middle-class gentlemen, and dinner at his private residence for the elite.

In four districts, though, Australia's first election day ended in violence and riots, including in Sydney and Melbourne. Police and soldiers struggled to control drunken mobs armed with staves and pickets who tore down banners, demolished campaign booths, and smashed the doors and windows of nearby shops and houses. Two men were killed, one in Sydney and one in a country district, and many injured. Irishmen were prominent among the rioters, giving the violence a sectarian edge, but alcohol and the attractions of mayhem were the main causes. There was nothing unusual in this by English precedent and Governor George Gipps reported back to London that 'The Election in general went off very well.'[2]

For the rest of the decade and into the 1850s the few elections held for the various colonies' Legislative Councils followed the English model. Henry Handel Richardson describes an election in Victoria after it had separated from New South Wales in her epic novel *The Fortunes of Richard Mahony* (1930). Mahony's brother-in-law, John Turnham, is standing for a Legislative Council seat in Ballarat in November 1855. It is not twelve months since the Eureka uprising, the mad defiant stand of rebellious diggers against the harsh enforcement of expensive mining licences by an often corrupt police which was brutally put down by the military. To pay for maintaining law and order on the goldfields the government had been charging miners eight pounds a year, and conducting regular police inspections. Many miners, barely making a living, were unlicensed. When the police arrived they fled, prompting cat-and-mouse hunts through the diggings.

In the wake of the rebellion, although a two-chamber parliament was soon to be established, eight new Legislative Council seats were created to give the goldfields immediate representation and the fictional Turnham is standing for one of these. A huge poster outside a pub offers free lunch to all men who register their vote for 'the one and only true democrat, the miners' friend and the tyrants' foe'. A crowd of roughs and loafers congregate at the entrance to the polling booth 'after the polite custom of the country to chivvy, or boo, or huzza those who went in'.

> Bands of music, one shriller and more discordant than the next, marched up and down the main streets—from the fife and drum

of the Fire Brigade to the kerosene-tins and penny-whistles of mere determined noise-makers. Straggling processions, with banners that bore the distorted features of one or other of the candidates, made driving difficult; and, to add to the confusion, the school children were let loose, to overrun the place and fly advertisement balloons round every corner.—And so it went on till far into the night, the dark hours being varied by torchlight processions, fireworks, free fights and orgies of drunkenness.

It is pandemonium. Similar scenes are repeated two days later when the results are announced. Turnham's acceptance speech can barely be heard above the cornet blown by a defeated opponent, and it ends in a general melee in which Turnham is injured. Through all this Turnham's sister Polly, though keenly interested in her brother's success, stays home. The rough and ready business of electioneering is no place for a lady.[3]

The election Richardson describes was the last Victorian election held according to the old ways. The Eureka rebellion at Ballarat and the harsh official response hastened a process of political reform already underway. In 1850 Victoria was separated from New South Wales, and by 1860 self-government had been granted to all the colonies except Western Australia, which still depended on convict labour. The various Legislative Councils drafted constitutions which were sent back to London by ship for modification and final parliamentary approval. Two-chamber parliaments were established, with the lower-house Legislative Assemblies elected on wider franchises than the upper-house Legislative Councils.

The English parliament also decided who would have the right to vote in colonial elections. Property, both owned and rented, remained the marker of the respectability and responsibility that made one fit to be an elector. There was no thought of giving the colonies manhood suffrage, but nonetheless during the 1850s it came about, almost accidentally and with little struggle.

The first accident was the contribution of a charming lawyer, Robert Lowe. Lowe was an albino with very poor eyesight. Early in 1842, when he was thirty-one, his doctors told him he would likely be blind in seven years. He decided to use his remaining years of light seeking his fortune in Australia and arrived at the end of the year. He was appointed to the New South Wales Legislative Council, where he became a champion of responsible government, an opponent of convict transportation and an advocate of state-supported non-denominational schools. But he was also a fierce defender of laissez-faire economics and implacably opposed to manhood suffrage.[4]

A brilliant lawyer and orator, Lowe did indeed make his fortune in Australia, returning to Britain in 1850, where he was on hand during debates about the new colonial constitutions. The New South Wales Legislative Council had recommended that the minimum property qualification be twenty pounds' rent per annum. This was too high, said Lowe. It would exclude respectable free immigrants yet to establish themselves and should be halved. Otherwise the electorate would be dominated by wealthy ex-convicts and their native-born children. Nothing was more likely to persuade Britain's rulers than fear of convict influence, and the House of Lords agreed. Ten pounds was the same as the British property qualification, which comfortably excluded most working men. They expected it would also do so in the colonies. But they were badly mistaken.[5]

The second accident was the discovery of gold in Victoria. Rents were already higher in the colonies than in Britain, especially in Sydney and Melbourne, and goldrush inflation soon pushed them higher still. In New South Wales the first constitution of 1855 also gave the vote to boarders paying forty pounds a year, to lodgers paying ten who had been at their residence for at least six months, and to men earning a salary of one hundred pounds. By 1856, when the first elections were held for the new Legislative Assembly, 63 per cent of adult men in the settled districts of New South Wales could vote and a whopping 95 per cent in Sydney. In England at the time only around 20 per cent of men could vote. In 1858 the new parliament in Sydney gave the vote to all men over twenty-one.[6]

In Victoria inflation was already expanding the electorate when the government gave the vote to diggers holding an annual mining licence. Introduced in the wake of Eureka, these cost a mere pound and virtually established manhood suffrage. In 1857 the first parliament abolished even these minimal qualifications. South Australia included manhood suffrage in its constitution. But in Tasmania, with its large population of ex-convicts, property qualifications lasted until 1900. Queensland and Western Australia also lagged behind the south-eastern mainland states. Queensland did not adopt manhood suffrage until 1872 and Western Australia waited until 1893, three years after it finally achieved self-government.[7]

These laggard colonies somewhat mar Australia's nineteenth-century democratic credentials, and there were other shortcomings. Manhood suffrage was only for the lower-house Assemblies. Property qualifications remained for Legislative Council elections in those states which had them, as well as plural voting, which gave electors a vote in every district in which they owned property. New South Wales and Queensland did not even have elections for their fully appointed Councils. Residency at one address for at least six months was required to register as a voter, which disenfranchised people who moved around a lot, including itinerant rural workers. Still, Australia was far ahead of Britain, where the dismantling of property qualifications was fought every step of the way until 1918, when the carnage of World War One made further resistance politically impossible. Forty per cent of the English, Scottish, Welsh and Irish men over twenty-one, the farm labourers and factory workers who could be conscripted and killed for their country, were still without the vote when they went to war.

Manhood suffrage was not the only item on the reformers' agenda in the 1850s when the new colonial parliaments were debating their foundational legislation. Many of the new immigrants' ideas about politics were shaped by Chartism, the great mid-century working-class movement, with its six demands for political reform: the vote for all men, payment of members of parliament, no property qualifications for parliamentarians, the secret ballot, equal electorates and annual elections. All except the last of these we now take for granted in healthy democracies.

Chartism was born in 1838, a year after the eighteen-year-old Princess Victoria became Queen of England. A group of political reformers drew up the People's Charter and its six demands quickly became the focal point of a working-class political movement which was launched in a series of huge open-air meetings the following year, mostly in England's north. The 1832 Reform Act had widened the franchise, given some representation to the fast-growing industrial towns and abolished the rotten boroughs (electorates where population decline had turned the parliamentary seat into the gift of the local landowner). But property was still the qualification to vote and the government showed no more concern for the lives of the working poor than before.

For those without the vote, parliament could be pressured to reform either by riot and uprisings, or by peaceful meetings, processions and petitions. There was some rioting, with swift reprisals, but mostly the Chartists relied on mass demonstrations of opinion to persuade the lawmakers to open up the parliament. The right to petition parliament was well established and the Chartists collected signatures for three monster petitions over the next decade: 1.3 million signatures in 1839 and three million in 1842. The number that signed the last, in 1848, was disputed. The Chartists claimed six million; the clerks of the House of Commons said it was only 1.9. Whatever the truth, the parliament was unmoved: 'Three and half millions have quietly, orderly, soberly, peaceably but firmly asked of their rulers to do justice; and their rulers have turned a deaf ear to that protest.'[8]

The 1840s were difficult years in Britain. The economy was stagnant, with few opportunities for the young, and in Ireland the potato famine killed up to a million people and forced as many again to sail for other shores. North America was the favoured destination of Britain's young emigrants, but some chose the three-month sea voyage to the bottom of the world. Between 1846 and 1851 Victoria's population more than doubled, from thirty-two thousand to seventy-seven thousand, and South Australia's tripled, to sixty-four thousand. With the discovery of gold at Ballarat in 1851, Victoria's population rose even faster, to 540,000 by 1861, an almost sixfold increase in a decade.[9]

These new arrivals had learned their politics during the 1830s and 1840s. Most were literate; many had participated in the Chartist movements and read the Chartist press; others had read the books, articles and pamphlets of philosophical radicals like Jeremy Bentham and James and John Stuart Mill, arguing that the power and privileges of the aristocracy were unjustifiable and that parliament had to become more representative. Perhaps in a new country, without the entrenched interests and privileges of the old world, truly representative political institutions could flourish.

In Britain the aristocracy had fought back against the 1832 Reform Act by using open voting to control the choices of their newly enfranchised tenants. Tenant farmers, local shopkeepers and village renters all risked retaliation if they voted against the landlord's candidate. Some few brave souls did defiantly call out the name of a rival candidate with the landlord's bailiff looking on, but most followed orders. Secret ballots were an easy way to limit the power of the landed aristocracy.

Defenders of the open ballot claimed a secret vote was 'un-English', not the forthright conduct expected of the sons of bluff John Bull. Secrecy was for women. Anthony Trollope, the finest novelist of mid-nineteenth-century English political life, wrote that it was 'unworthy of a great people to free itself from the evil results of vicious conduct by unmanly restraints'.[10] These claims had a sectarian edge. The manly English character displayed in open voting was a decidedly Protestant construct, hostile to the secrecy of the Catholic confessional and the feminine dependence of Catholics on their priests.[11]

In Australia, the achievement of near-universal manhood suffrage in the most populous colonies inverted the political dynamics of arguments about secret voting. Faced with a wave of working-class voters, conservatives argued that secrecy was needed to protect them from the intimidation of the radical masses. Melbourne's conservative newspaper, the *Argus*, became an advocate of the secret ballot as a protection against the excesses of democracy: 'It would be of little use to escape the evil influence of landlords and masters, to fall beneath the yoke of a tyrant majority.'[12]

Majoritarian democracy has always competed with the rights of minorities. Today we most often associate the defence of minority rights with progressive causes such as support for racial or sexual minorities, but there is nothing inherently progressive in it. The rich and powerful will always be a minority. During Australia's recent marriage-equality debate, some supporters of traditional marriage argued that they needed to be protected from the bullying of the politically correct majority.

Victoria was the first Australian colony to make voting secret. The new constitution establishing responsible parliamentary government for the colony arrived in October 1855, and it allowed the Legislative Council to formulate the rules for the forthcoming elections. William Haines, the colony's chief secretary, prepared a bill following the existing British practice of open voting, but others wanted a secret ballot. Another councillor, William Nicholson, a successful grocer and former mayor of Melbourne, moved that the elections be conducted by secret ballot. It would prevent voter intimidation, he argued, particularly by the government, which was a very large employer; and it would stop the practice of treating and so make elections more orderly. No one would bother to buy a voter a drink, he said, if they couldn't check whether he kept his side of the bargain. Hence there would be less drinking and so less chance of drunken disorder. The motion was passed, thirty-three to twenty-five, against the wishes of the government of the day, and Haines resigned.

Haines's government was subsequently reinstated before the election, but it refused to implement the parliament's wishes for a secret ballot to be incorporated into the Electoral Act. At this point no one had a clear idea of how a secret ballot would actually work, so advocates needed someone to draft a practical working proposal which could be incorporated in legislation. Henry Chapman, another member of the Legislative Council, offered himself for the task, and was gratefully accepted.[13]

Chapman was one of the legions of energetic middle-class men who kept the British empire turning. In his twenties, while working in Quebec as an export and import agent, he had immersed himself in the writings of the philosophical radicals led by Jeremy Bentham and James Mill. He started writing himself and founded a radical newspaper. When he supported the French Catholic minority's demands for parliamentary representation, English merchants stopped advertising in his paper and it folded. He returned to England, where he held various salaried administrative positions, read for the bar and continued to write about political reform. In 1843, when he was forty, he was appointed as a judge in New Zealand and in 1852 the British colonial secretary, Earl Grey, appointed him colonial secretary of Van Diemen's Land. It was a brief tenure. Van Diemen's Land had a partly elected Legislative Council, and when the elected members passed a motion to end convict transportation, Chapman supported them against the views of the overbearing lieutenant governor, Sir William Denison, and was dismissed.[14]

Chapman supported the elected legislative councillors not only because he too opposed transportation but also because he believed in responsible government: that policy should be made by local elected representatives, not by the faraway Crown and its appointed men. He was subsequently offered other positions, including the governorship of the West Indies, but he declined them all and instead went to the Victorian Bar just a few months before the diggers' uprising at Eureka. In February 1855 he stood for the Legislative Council at a by-election. Though a newcomer, his manly refusal to 'flinch from his duty before the frown of a mere convict-loving autocrat' was well known across Bass Strait, and he easily won the ballot. Together with his solid liberal credentials, he was welcomed for the usefulness of his administrative experience and knowledge of official routines which too often baffled the businessmen and merchants on the Council.[15]

So when Haines's law officers were refusing to draft legislation for the secret ballot, and its major advocate William Nicholson had no practical ideas, Chapman and his administrative experience saved the day. By then he had another liberal feather in his cap. Just weeks after he was elected to the Legislative Council he successfully defended the African-American Eureka rebel John Joseph against charges of treason.

It was a pro bono defence, for where the American consul assisted the other arrested American citizens, it did not help Joseph.[16]

Chapman began with Jeremy Bentham's suggestion in his 1819 *Radical Reform Bill* that the voter should arrive at the polling booth empty-handed, rather than bringing his already filled-out voting paper with him, which as likely as not had been provided by one of the candidates. All the materials he needed to vote would be supplied to him, and the government would bear the cost.

Secret voting already existed in France, Belgium, Switzerland and many American states, but the method was different. Voters brought their own voting papers to the polling place and put them in the ballot box, which had replaced the polling books in which each elector's vote was publicly recorded. They were not asked to name their preferred candidate or to sign their ballot, but if they voted on papers supplied by the candidate and in the candidate's colours their preference was obvious.[17] In the United States the parties provided voters with distinctively coloured voting cards already filled in. All the voter had to do was drop the card in the box and anyone could check the colour.

The novel part of Chapman's plan was not the secrecy itself but the means by which the secrecy was achieved: the government-provided ballot paper. Traditionally governments would issue the writs, but otherwise not be involved in running elections. It was left to the candidates and their committees or parties, or to the voters themselves, to organise ballot papers. All the polling booth needed was a ballot box to put them in. Now the government would oversee the whole operation. The printed ballot papers listed the names of the candidates, and voters crossed out those they rejected. This made it easy for those who had difficulty writing. Those who couldn't read could vote if someone told them which lines to strike out—'every line after the first', for example, or 'all except second from the bottom'. They could also ask for assistance, as could the blind.

But Chapman's plan required further innovation. How and where was the ballot paper to be filled in? What would prevent the watchful eyes of the candidates' electoral agents from checking how people voted? Chapman's proposal was this. The voter would pick up a ballot from the polling clerk, who would mark his name off the roll and sign the back of his ballot to prevent fraud. The voter would then pass into an inner room where he would vote in private, with pen, ink and blotting paper provided. He would then return to the polling clerk and put his folded ballot in the box.

When the bill mandating Chapman's proposed method was debated in the Legislative Council, opponents, thinking to kill it off, pointed out how long this process would take at a busy booth: at least three minutes per voter. Only twenty men would be able to vote in an hour. But this objection was met with a further innovation, suggested in fact by an opponent of secret voting, Charles Griffith. Why not have five or six stalls or compartments in the inner room? This idea was added to the bill, along with another innovation: alphabetical divisions in the outer room to speed up the issuing of ballot papers.

Eventually, and with great reluctance, the government adopted the system for the election in 1856 of Victoria's first parliament. The returning officers were provided with detailed plans for their polling stations and all the materials they would need: pens, ink, blotting paper, ballot boxes and boards to construct the stalls, which were to be four foot wide and eight foot high, separated with boards an inch thick. The invention of the voting stalls, says John Hirst, was just as crucial to the success of the scheme as the ballot paper. Together, these practical measures made secret voting a workable reality. It is often said that Australia invented the secret ballot. This is somewhat misleading, as it was already in place elsewhere. What Australia pioneered were new and more efficient means to implement it.

All went smoothly at this first trial. Election day was quieter and more orderly than in the past, with thinner crowds and less treating, though there was still some. Candidates and their committees checked that those who had promised their support actually turned up to vote, and stood them a drink when they did. The big difference was that the returning officer no longer kept and posted a running tally. No one would know the result until the ballot box was unlocked at the end of the day and the votes were counted. This ended the mad rush in close elections to round up the drunken stragglers. Opponents of the secret ballot dropped their objections. A few years later the public nomination of candidates on the hustings was replaced with paper forms. The only remaining public election event was the announcement of the results, when large crowds would gather around tally boards outside newspaper offices, singing, cheering and booing.[18]

Tasmania and South Australia adopted almost identical systems to Victoria at about the same time, and New South Wales and Queensland a few years later. South Australia made two innovations to speed things up in the voting stall. With the dipping pen, even men used to writing took up to five minutes to complete their vote, and many took much longer, so electors were instead provided with pencils. And voters no longer put a line through the names of rejected candidates, but instead put a cross in a square next to their preferred candidate. These reforms were later adopted for Commonwealth elections.

The official printed ballot paper and the compartments for voting became known as the Australian ballot, and attracted the interest of reformers in Britain and the United States. In Britain it was seen as a way to reduce the power of the landed gentry and to free elections from intimidation, riot and drunken disorder; in the United States it was hoped it would limit the control of party machines. It was adopted in New Zealand in 1870 and the United Kingdom in 1872, after the colonial premiers had testified to enquiring British parliamentarians of its success. The House of Lords, however, took some convincing, and rejected secret-ballot legislation twenty-eight times before finally relenting.[19] The Australian ballot then spread through Europe, the Canadian provinces and the American states, though each polity made its own minor variations.

The Australian ballot turned voting into a well-mannered civic ritual. A pamphlet from the English Ballot Society in the 1860s contrasts the rowdy chaos of open elections with the quiet order of elections in the Australian colonies. In the ruckus in front of the English open polling booth, men exchange punches and an urchin picks a man's pocket. In Australia, electors line up in their separate compartments, silently recording their votes. Respectable English folk liked to believe the colonies were rough places, peopled by the uncouth descendants of convicts. The Australian ballot proved otherwise.

3

THREE SOUTH AUSTRALIAN INNOVATORS

SOUTH AUSTRALIA WAS invaded by Europeans at about the same time as Victoria, but its beginnings were very different. Rather than sealers along the coast and unauthorised Vandemonians crossing Bass Strait in search of land, with plenty of ex-convicts among them, South Australia was created by an act of the British parliament. As a colony of free settlers it would provide good returns for investors and work for fertile young couples from the old country. Care was taken that the number of women emigrants equalled men. Not only would women bear and raise the children, but their civilising presence would balance the rough masculinity of the frontier. And there would be no established church, making early South Australia a haven for religious dissenters, including German-speaking Lutherans escaping oppression in Prussia. This convict-free colony of dissenters provides two of our story's heroines and one of its heroes: Catherine Helen Spence, Mary Lee and William Boothby.

South Australia became self-governing in 1856, and began the establishment of the institutions of responsible parliament. Like other colonies, it had a Legislative Assembly elected on manhood suffrage and a Legislative Council with a more restricted franchise. The votes were counted by the tried and true British method of first-past-the-post. This was the method used when electors told a returning officer their preferred candidate, and it was simply transferred to the secret paper ballot. It was also transferred to multi-member electorates in a system called the block vote, in which voters have as many votes as there are representatives to be elected, and those with the most votes win. If there are five positions to be filled, a voter has five votes, although they may or may not be obliged to use them all.

First-past-the-post is a winner-takes-all system. To be sure, victory goes to the candidate with the most votes, but not necessarily with the support of the majority of the electorate. Say the vote falls like this: A, 15 per cent; B, 15 per cent; C, 20 per cent; D, 35 per cent; and E, 15 per cent. D is clearly the winner, with the majority of votes, but 65 per cent of the electorate voted for someone else. The views of substantial minorities are excluded, especially in the block-voting system for multi-member electorates. A well-organised minority which runs a solid ticket against a scattered field can win all the available seats, leaving not only the majority unrepresented but also the views of other sizeable minorities. The challenge for mid-nineteenth-century electoral reformers was how to balance the desirability of majority support for governments with the representation of minority interests. It was a challenge taken up by Catherine Spence.

Spence arrived in South Australia aged fourteen with her parents in 1839, just three years after the new colony's official proclamation. This Scottish lass grew into a remarkable Australian woman who well deserves her portrait on our five-dollar note. Confident, whip-smart and brimming with energy, she threw herself into many causes in her long life: the care of destitute children, kindergartens, girls' education, votes for women and electoral reform. In 1854 she became the first woman to publish a novel about Australia—a Jane Austen-style love story entitled *Clara Morison: A Tale of South Australia During the Gold Fever*. She published more novels, but her true metier was journalism and public debate, and she was already writing for her brother-in-law's newspaper when *Clara Morison* was published.

The Spence family were omnivorous readers with a keen interest in the development of the new colony. 'We took hold of the growth and development of South Australia, and identified ourselves with it. Nothing is insignificant in the development of a young community, and—above all—nothing seems impossible,' she wrote in her autobiography many years later. In 1859 she read a review by John Stuart Mill in *Fraser's Magazine* of three recent publications on parliamentary reform. One was by Thomas Hare: 'A Treatise on the Election of Representatives, Parliamentary and Municipal'. Its ideas electrified her. A lawyer committed to political reform who moved in the same circles as Mill, Hare had devised a system of voting which would give some representation to minorities. It showed Spence 'how democratic government could be made real, safe and progressive', and 'the reform of the electoral system became the foremost object of my life.'[1]

Thomas Hare's system used the single transferable vote to elect a chamber where the parties' seats correspond to the number of votes cast for them: hence the term 'proportional representation'. Voters each have a single vote that is initially given to their most preferred candidate. Successful candidates must get a quota, with excess votes transferred to the next preferred candidate, and so on, until all votes are allocated. Many European elections also aim for proportional representation, but they achieve it differently, by a simple matching of the proportion of votes in the electorate with the proportion of elected representatives in the legislature, without the chance for voters to express their individual preferences.

Hare initially treated the whole of Great Britain as one electorate returning 645 candidates, proposing to discard the local single-member electorates which were the basis of its parliamentary representation. This severed the links between members of parliament and their constituents. Which of the 645 MPs would an aggrieved elector complain to about the route of a new road? And who would open the local fete? Hare's proposal never got off the ground, but the idea of proportional representation appealed to reformers as a way to loosen the grip of the aristocracy and landed gentry on parliament, and to give a chance to men from the industrial towns. John Stuart Mill promoted it, and societies formed for its propagation.[2]

When Spence first read of Hare's scheme, the block-voting system had just delivered a labour political association victory in five of six seats in the Assembly for the multi-member electorate of Adelaide without obtaining a majority of votes, as well as all three seats in the electorates of Burra and Clare. Hare's system was addressing just this type of outcome. Spence was the Adelaide correspondent for the Melbourne *Argus*, writing under her brother's name. The night after she read Mill's review she wrote an article on Hare's system and sent it off: 'I knew that the *Argus* was dissatisfied with the elections,' and 'fancied that the editor would hail with joy the new idea'. But the editor replied that the *Argus* was committed to the representation of majorities and would not even print her piece as a letter.[3]

In 1861 Spence wrote 'A Plea for Pure Democracy', a pamphlet urging that Hare's method be used for elections to the South Australian Legislative Assembly to ensure that the views of minorities were represented.[4] Her ideas were largely ignored and she moved on to other causes, but in the early 1890s, with labour organising and federation in the offing, her passion for electoral reform rekindled. 'Proportional representation,' she believed, 'was the hope of the world.'[5]

Now in her late sixties, Spence took to the public platform to argue for it. She modified Hare's scheme to apply to multi-member electorates of nine to ten members and called it effective voting, and would hold mock elections at her lectures to show people how it worked. It would ensure that all groups, including labour, would have some representation, but she also believed that it would counter the development of powerful party organisations in which independent thought would be disciplined out of existence and co-operative reform become harder to achieve.

Never having married or borne children, Spence was in better health than most women of her age, but it took courage to face the hecklers and risk scorn and insult from the assembled men. Arguing that proportional representation should be adopted for the new federation, she stood for the 1897 federal convention. She was Australia's first woman political candidate, and like those who followed in the Commonwealth's early years she was unsuccessful. But her campaign put electoral methods on the agenda for the new Commonwealth.[6]

In Tasmania, another political reformer of Scottish descent, Andrew Inglis Clark, was also persuaded by Hare's ideas. Born in Hobart, Clark became a barrister and politician with a deep interest in constitutional history. Unlike Spence, Clark was a man with power, so he wasn't limited to platform persuasion. As the colony's attorney-general he could act on his beliefs, and he took up Spence's idea of applying Hare's scheme to multi-member electorates for Tasmania's 1896 Legislative Assembly elections. He argued that, with the block system currently in place, a majority of voters would select all the parliamentarians and a very large minority would be totally unrepresented. Under his scheme, however, 'every section of political opinion which can command the requisite quota of votes' could be represented. He slightly modified the way the quota was calculated and preferences distributed, and his scheme became known as the Clark-Hare and then as the Hare-Clark system. It was used for Tasmanian elections until the end of the century, dropped for a short return to first-past-the-post, then reintroduced in 1907, where it has stayed for state elections.[7]

Colonial Queensland also experimented with a different voting system. In 1892 Queensland introduced what was then called the Contingent Vote for elections to the lower house. By the end of the nineteenth century second ballots, or runoffs between the two top candidates, were used in the United States and some European countries, and this is what the Queensland government had in mind, but it was expensive and administratively difficult to hold a second election, especially in the large outback electorates. With ballot papers it was possible to compress the runoff system into a single shot. Voters only had to turn up once to the polling place but were given the option of expressing a preference should their number-one candidate not win. A runoff was then held between the top two candidates by the distribution of preferences from the other candidates.

This is a simplified version of the preferential system Australia uses in contemporary elections for the House of Representatives and all the state lower houses, except in Tasmania. If no candidate receives an absolute majority on first count, the preferences of the other candidates are distributed until one candidate has more than 50 per cent of the vote. Whether or not preferences are optional or compulsory and the way preferences are distributed vary. The details get very technical, but the aim of the system is majoritarian. It produces the candidate who is least disliked, the one the majority is most prepared to live with.[8] This is how the Sydney independent Kerryn Phelps defeated the Liberal Party candidate, Dave Sharma, at the Wentworth by-election in 2018. Phelps had only 29.19 per cent of the first-preference vote to Sharma's

43.08, but after the preferences of the fourteen other candidates were distributed she had 51.22 per cent of the two-party-preferred vote.[9]

Australia's preferential voting at both state and federal level is another distinctive feature of our electoral system. But, unlike the Australian ballot, few countries have followed. Most still use first-past-the-post. Preferential voting is used in Ireland and Sri Lanka for presidential elections, and in Canada, the United States and the United Kingdom for some local or regional elections. Otherwise the only other countries to take it up are in the Pacific region.[10] As we will see, it was resisted fiercely when included in the first Commonwealth Electoral Bill, in 1902. The government had to drop it, but the idea did not go away.

Our South Australian hero, William Boothby, came to the colony in 1853, the eldest of twelve surviving siblings, when his father, Benjamin, was appointed as one of two judges to the Supreme Court on relatively limited legal experience. Benjamin Boothby's was the last appointment the Colonial Office made to the South Australian bench and it was not a happy one. Although a dissenter and a radical Chartist in his younger days, by the time of his appointment he had become a quarrelsome conservative, a self-righteous pedant with little sympathy for the colonists' desires for legal autonomy. His term was a disaster, and after thirteen years of conflict with leading politicians and lawyers he was removed from his position. His greatest contribution to South Australia was his eldest son.[11]

William Boothby was twenty-four when he arrived in Adelaide with a Bachelor of Arts from the University of London. We don't know exactly what subjects he studied, but the London curriculum was far more modern than that of Classics-dominated Oxford and Cambridge. The university was also much cheaper, with no barriers to admission of race, religion or political belief. Oxbridge's requirement that students be members of the Church of England made it off-limits for dissenters and Catholics. Likely William read the work of political reformers like Bentham and the Mills, with their many practical suggestions for making government more representative; and he already had an interest in elections and some practical experience, having served as secretary in a hotly contested election in Yorkshire.[12]

When the Boothbys arrived in Adelaide it was gripped by the gold fever which Spence describes in *Clara Morison*. With the town emptied of so many of its able men, this well-educated new arrival slid smoothly into the position of the colony's deputy sheriff when the sheriff, Charles Newenham, was on a trip Home. When Newenham resigned in 1856, Boothby became sheriff, and held the post till his death in 1903. Just a few months after Boothby was promoted, in October 1856, South Australia achieved responsible government and he was given the task of running the first elections under the new constitution.

What a challenge for a bright young man only two years into the job, the green fields of a new colony stretching before him, unencumbered by time-honoured ways of doing things and without entrenched vested interests. There were, though, some fences already in place, erected by the 1856 Electoral Act. Nominations were by paper, not on the hustings; voting was by paper ballot; and polling booths were not to be 'in a house licensed for the sale of wine, beer or spirituous liquors or within one hundred yards of same'.[13]

As well, the government would bear the cost of the elections, not the candidates or the electors. In Britain elections cost the government almost nothing. Electors paid a shilling a year to be on the electoral roll, which paid the returning officer, and the candidates hired the venues where the nomination and polling took place. In shifting the cost to the government, South Australia was following the lead of New South

Wales, which abolished all costs to electors and candidates in 1843, thus proving to the British just how extravagant the colonists were.

South Australia also shifted the management of the electoral rolls to salaried government officials. In England local council officers compiled and maintained electoral rolls, and disputes were settled by local magistrates. But South Australia in 1856 had a scattered population of barely a hundred thousand Europeans, no local government officers, no postmasters, no local magistrates and only a rudimentary police force. So the task of managing the rolls was added to the duties of the returning officers for the various electoral districts.

In Britain returning officers were temporary appointments for the duration of an election; in South Australia they became permanent government positions. This was a momentous development, the first step in our proud history of non-partisan electoral administration which has kept parties and politicians away from the management of elections, something Americans can only dream of.

There was one more significant innovation: the creation of the position of Provincial Returning Officer. The South Australian constitution established a Legislative Assembly based on single-member electorates, each with a divisional returning officer, and a Legislative Council with a single province-wide electoral district and one Provincial Returning Officer. William Boothby was the first incumbent, and he turned it into a powerful co-ordinating authority and a source of expert advice to government on electoral matters.

His advice began with a series of recommendations he made after the 1856 election that were incorporated into a revised act in 1858. His most famous was 'the cross within the square', a redesigned ballot paper which replaced the often laborious crossing out of names with a simple cross in a box, a great saving in both ink and time. He also regularised the duties and the payment of the District Returning Officers. In the 1856 act they were paid a fixed sum plus an uncapped reimbursement of expenses. Unsurprisingly, costs blew out, so he replaced this with a fixed annual sum.

At first the District Returning Officers retained some autonomy, but in 1896 the Provincial Returning Officer got full power over them, setting up a clear chain of command. Here was another colonial innovation: a powerful central office overseeing a colony-wide electoral machinery, not unlike the Election Master General which Bentham had recommended in his *Radical Reform Bill*, and a precursor of the Chief Electoral Officer established by the first Commonwealth Electoral Act in 1902.

As the Provincial Returning Officer, Boothby turned his bureaucrat's mind to rationalising the management of the electoral rolls. First, he recommended replacing annual with continuous enrolment. This meant that returning officers worked throughout year, albeit part-time.

Second, he introduced a modicum of co-ordination among government agencies, requiring the registrar of births, deaths and marriages to inform returning officers of electors' deaths, and instituting a system to transfer electors' names from one district to another when they moved.

Third, compiling the roll became the responsibility of the government, whereas before it had been up to eligible voters to apply to have their names put on it. Boothby had local council clerks and police officers deliver enrolment forms to every habitation in the colony, a massive undertaking requiring many hours in the saddle. This was repeated every five years until the end of the century, when the habitation review was conducted at the same time as the census. Voters still had to fill in and return their forms. On Boothby's advice this was mandatory. After a few years the government dropped the compulsion, in part because too many people claimed they had never received the forms, but the spirit of compulsion was already there, hampered only by practical considerations. Tellingly, there was no philosophical repulsion from mandatory enrolment.[14]

The roll shrank considerably when it was no longer mandatory to register. Boothby had been against dropping the compulsion, and many now agreed with him that its removal had been a mistake, but it was not restored. Boothby's advocacy foreshadowed the role that electoral officers would play in Australia's journey to compulsory voting. On one electoral matter, though, Boothby supported the way things had always been done. He was entirely unconvinced by Catherine Spence's arguments for proportional representation. It would, he said, be unintelligible to the average voter.[15]

In the middle of the nineteenth century, South Australia developed the first permanent electoral administration in the world, overseen by a Chief Electoral Officer whose position and salary were set by legislation: Jeremy Bentham's Election Master General made flesh in William Robinson Boothby, who combined Bentham's energetic commitment to reform with close attention to administrative detail. This story is less well known than that of the Australian ballot, but it similarly shows Australians' untroubled confidence in government, especially if it will bear the cost of providing a public good like an election, and our penchant for uniform bureaucratic solutions.[16]

Boothby suggested one more innovation: voting through the post as a cheaper alternative for the outlying districts than providing polling stations for every remote location. This was the first publicly expressed plan for voting away from the ballot box, but it was not taken up. The secret ballot had only just been achieved and postal voting threatened to reopen opportunities for bribery and coercion.[17] The cost was the disenfranchisement of people in the backblocks, many of whom were just the sort of conservative rural voters on whom governments relied.

In 1877 Western Australia introduced postal voting for people living more than thirty miles from a polling booth, or who would be outside their district on election day. South Australia introduced similar provisions in 1890, and Victoria in 1899. Provisions for obtaining and returning postal votes were elaborate, both to protect secrecy and to prevent fraud, and varied among the states, but at least they were available. As we will see, the newly formed Labor Party was trenchantly opposed to postal voting and abolished it as soon as it got the chance.

South Australia's final electoral innovation is the best known of all: giving the vote to women in 1894, second in the world after New Zealand the year before. Women ratepayers had been able to vote in South Australian local government elections since 1861, as had their Victorian ratepaying sisters since 1854, but not those who owned no property.

During the 1880s a determined and well-organised women's suffrage movement developed across the English-speaking world, driven by respectable middle-class women committed to moral and social reform and to temperance. 'Social' was a euphemism for 'sexual', and suffragists argued that women needed the vote to pressure male-dominated parliaments to legislate to protect women and children from vice and degradation by sexually licentious men. They also wanted governments to restrict the sale of alcohol, a major cause of violence against women and children and a blight on many family budgets.

From today's perspective these campaigning women are a contradictory mix of progressive faith in women's rights and strident wowserism. But their campaign for the vote was hard-fought, and their moral concerns gave many suffragists the conviction to keep going in the face of scorn and repeated obstruction. Others were simply committed to women becoming full citizens and democratic participants.

During the 1880s and 1890s, sympathetic men regularly introduced bills into the colonial parliaments to give women the vote, and they were just as regularly blocked by threatened men defending the privileges of male pleasure and power. Arguments ranged from the patronising (sensitive, gentle women should be protected from the dirty world of politics), to the insulting (women are too stupid, ignorant or flippant to follow the arguments), to the offensive (who wants to be told what to do by a bunch of petticoats?).[18] But there was also widespread support. By the mid-1890s the labour movement supported the adult franchise, as did the majority of progressive liberals, who regarded the arguments for women's democratic participation as incontrovertible.

In South Australia the campaign was led by Mary Lee, the plump, energetic widow of an Irish clergyman who had come to the colony in 1879 when she was fifty-eight. She joined the Social Purity Society which campaigned successfully to raise the age of consent to sixteen, but concluded that the suffrage was essential if women's social and sexual status was to be further improved. In 1888 she inaugurated the Women's Suffrage League and became its honorary secretary. The president was Edward Stirling who, in 1886, had introduced a bill to enfranchise women into the South Australian parliament. Catherine Spence was the vice-president.

For the next eight years Mary Lee campaigned tirelessly, addressing meetings, writing letters and articles for the press, lobbying politicians, and organising petitions to parliament. Like the Chartists before them, the suffragists collected signatures for monster petitions. In Victoria in 1891 suffragists collected thirty thousand signatures. Lee organised a petition of 11,600 signatures in 1894, just a few months before the South Australian parliament finally gave women the right to vote.[19] Their Victorian sisters had to wait another fourteen years, till 1908.

Catherine Spence arrived back in Adelaide the week before the suffragists' victory, after twenty months abroad promoting the case for effective voting, as well as speaking on the state care of children and on the female suffrage. She had begun her travels at the 1893 World Fair in Chicago, where she was everywhere greeted with 'You come from Australia, the home of the secret ballot.'[20] On Monday evening, 17 December 1894, she was welcomed home at the Café de Paris on Rundle Street by a room full of excited women and a few men. The suffrage bill was on the brink of success and many had come straight from the House, where the debate was in full flight.

All day women had crowded into the chamber to hear the debate. Mary Lee observed that 'those with the least to say took the longest time to say it' but that 'every man had a right to a free mother and a free wife.' Spence, who had just turned sixty-nine, hoped that 'before she was too decrepit she would be able to go to the poll and record her vote'. She looked forward to a time when women would have their fair share of power, and when all shades of opinion would have a hearing in the legislature.[21] Although she rejoiced that women were finally to attain the vote, she still gave a higher priority to effective voting, failing to see 'the advantage of having a vote that might leave me after an election a disenfranchised voter, instead of an unenfranchised woman'.[22] It was an eccentric position.

Next day, hoping to sabotage the bill, the conservatives introduced an amendment: not only would women be able to vote, they would be able to stand as candidates. The suffragists hadn't asked for this and conservatives thought it was so patently absurd that the bill would be lost. But they were wrong. Just before midnight on Tuesday, 18 December 1894, the bill, with the conservatives' amendment, passed, thirty-one votes to fourteen. 'The Ayes were sonorous and cheery, the Noes despondent like muffled bells,' observed one reporter. One No shouted at the Ayes, 'Not half of you will get back next time'; another yelled, as cheering broke out from the galleries, 'There's the hen's convention.' But the Ayes had it, and South Australia became the first place in the world to give women the right to stand for parliament as well as to vote.[23]

At the next South Australian election women were out in force. It was Saturday, 25 April 1896, a fine day across the colony. Election days had been a bit drab since the end of open voting, but now polling places were buzzing with excitement as the clerks struggled to accommodate so many new voters. Yet it was healthy excitement, nothing like the riotous drunken behaviour of old. The Adelaide *Observer* felt that the presence of women made for a calmer, more decorous atmosphere, and that the men were generally quieter and more thoughtful. At North Adelaide the black-and-white-garbed sisters of the Dominican Convent solemnly followed their Mother Superior into the Temperance Hall, 'grave, kindly and silent'. Ladies in their Sunday best rolled up in cabs or came on foot. Some were grave with their new responsibilities; some were nervous, edging into the hall like crabs; and a few marched in with a determined masculine stride, exemplifying what the opponents of female suffrage had feared. Later that night, many women were in the crowds watching the results going up on the tally board outside the *Observer*'s office, claiming their new occupancy of political space. When the vote was counted, it was found that the informal rate was unusually low, a vindication of South Australia's latest experiment with democracy.[24]

Three years later, in August 1899, Western Australia also gave the vote to women, though the reasons were more ambivalent. Western Australia had only been self-governing since 1890. Its population was a mere forty-six thousand, and power was in the hands of a tightly knit elite of pastoralists and city merchants. So why was this small conservative backwater the second colony to adopt such a progressive reform? The answer is simple: after the discovery of huge deposits of gold in Kalgoorlie and Coolgardie in the early 1890s, a rush of diggers from the eastern states with radical political ideas shifted the balance of the population away from Perth and the farming districts in the south-west corner of the state. The politicians hoped that giving women the vote would help them retain power by rebalancing the electorates. Women were scarce on the goldfields, and far less likely to vote for Labor candidates.[25]

By the late 1890s, federation was finally close and with it the possibility that all Australian women would get the vote, for federal elections at least. The document that would become the Constitution of the Commonwealth of Australia was debated, clause by clause, at conventions in 1897 and 1898, attended by elected delegates from Victoria, New South Wales, South Australia and Tasmania. Queensland was remaining aloof, and the West Australian delegates were selected by their parliament.

Previous federal councils and conventions had met in Melbourne, Sydney and Hobart. The 1897 convention met in Adelaide. The city of churches was not a popular choice with the men from Victoria and New South Wales, too staid and quiet for their anticipated pleasures, but the premier, Charles Kingston, had the support of Western Australia and Tasmania. For the West Australians, still deciding whether to come, it had the advantage of being closer to home and sealed their participation.[26] It was a propitious decision for Australian women's right to vote. Whether or not adult suffrage would be included in the new constitution would be debated in this city of confident, enfranchised women who now had the power to derail the federal project.

South Australian women would vote in the referendum on the constitution. If it looked like federation would disenfranchise them, they and their male supporters might vote No and jeopardise the birth of the new nation. South Australia was rightly proud of its early achievement of adult suffrage, the unrestricted right of every adult over twenty-one to vote. The sky had not fallen in: pubs still sold beer to thirsty men, and women still cooked their families' meals and shared their husbands' beds. On the other hand, if it looked like federation would impose female suffrage everywhere, the male electors in other states might vote No.

The South Australian Women's Suffrage League had a petition ready for the convention when it opened, requesting that the constitution include adult suffrage 'so that a united Australia may become a true democracy, resting upon the will of the whole people, and not half the people'. Suffragists in the other colonies added their voices and each day women crowded in to watch the debates taking place in South Australia's parliament. Former premier Frederick Holder, whose wife, Julia, was a committed suffragist and close friend of Mary Lee, proposed that adult suffrage be written into the constitution. This was too much for most of the delegates, so Holder tried a different tack. The new parliament would determine the franchise, but the constitution would include a clause which read, 'No adult person who has or acquires a right to vote at elections for the more numerous Houses of the Parliament of a State shall, while the right continues, be prevented by any law of the Commonwealth from voting at elections for either House of the Parliament of the Commonwealth.'[27]

This became section 41. It was designed to reassure South Australians that women's voting rights would be protected, without actually saying so directly. Combined with the commitment that the franchise would be the same in every state, it seemed to guarantee that the new nation would allow all of its adults to vote.

4

DIRECTLY CHOSEN BY THE PEOPLE

THE NEW COMMONWEALTH of Australia was inaugurated along with the new century on 1 January 1901, at a grand outdoor ceremony in Sydney's Centennial Park. With the crowds of onlookers and imperial troops sweltering under the early afternoon sun, the clerk of the Federation Convention, the South Australian Edwin Blackmore, read Queen Victoria's proclamation of the new Commonwealth. The old queen had just a few more weeks to live. When she ascended to the throne in 1837 there were only two Australian colonies, New South Wales and Tasmania. Now there were six, two of them named after her, beginning their new life together as states in a federation.

The governor-general, Lord Hopetoun, then swore in a ministry. Hopetoun had had a torrid couple of weeks since he arrived on 15 December 1900, weak from typhoid fever, and invited the premier of New South Wales, William Lyne, to form a ministry. Everyone had expected Hopetoun to choose Edmund Barton, and he and his allies refused to serve with Lyne. On Christmas Eve, with the inauguration ceremony only a week away, Lyne returned his commission and Hopetoun sent for Barton.

Barton formed a ministry of big men with extensive experience in colonial politics, premiers and ex-premiers like the West Australian John Forrest; the Victorian George Turner; William Lyne, still smarting from losing the prime ministership; and Barton's close friend and ally in the deposing of Lyne, Victoria's silver-tongued orator Alfred Deakin. This cabinet of kings would comprise an interim government until a general election could be held for the new parliament.

The constitution did not specify who could vote in the new Commonwealth: the franchise would be left to the new parliament to determine. But it did lay down some clear parameters. First (as specified in sections 7 and 24), both houses were to be 'directly chosen by the people'. The first version of the constitution in 1891 had provided for direct elections by the people to the lower house but had baulked at a democratically elected Senate. Instead, senators were to be elected by the various state parliaments.

The requirement that both houses be 'directly chosen by the people' is a major difference between Australia's federal political institutions and those of the United States, on which they were modelled. Until 1914 American senators were elected by state legislatures, and the president is still elected indirectly. People vote for members of an electoral college, which then elects the president.

The Australian Senate was designed to be a states' house, with equal representation from each state so that the interests of the smaller states like Tasmania and South Australia would not be trampled by the much larger populations of Victoria and New South Wales. But it would also be the upper house in a two-chamber parliament, a house to review the government's legislation. The upper houses of the colonial parliaments were designed to be conservative, to protect the status quo from sudden impulses of popular feeling and to check the feared excesses of the unschooled poor. So they were given a more restricted franchise than the lower-house assemblies and in some colonies included members directly appointed by the governor. Time and again in the nineteenth century upper houses fulfilled their conservative mission and blocked reforming legislation.

If the Senate was to be a conservative house of review, it too would need to be elected differently from the lower house. As John Hirst observes, during the nineteenth century 'An upper house elected on a democratic franchise was almost a contradiction in terms.' The authors of the 1891 draft constitution knew it would be politically difficult, if not impossible, to restrict the Senate's franchise without scuttling the federal project. Instead they proposed indirect election. State senators would be chosen by the state parliaments. This would make the Senate responsible to the state parliaments rather than directly to the people and so provide a likely conservative check to a more radical lower house.

But this method did not survive. Democrats had two reasons to reject the proposed Senate. The first was that because the colonies' populations were so uneven, and likely to remain so, a Tasmanian senator would represent far fewer electors than would a senator from Victoria or New South Wales. The second was that the people would not be directly electing the Senate. It was impossible to compromise on the first reason and hold the smaller colonies in the federation, but democrats won the second. At the conventions in the late 1890s, when the constitution was redrafted before it was put to the people, indirect election to the Senate was quietly dropped. Instead the constitution specified that both houses were to be 'directly chosen by the people'.[1]

The constitution also specified that the electoral law for choosing senators was to be 'uniform' for all states (section 9). The word appears often in the debates on the constitution and in the early years of the

Commonwealth, with a meaning that has largely fallen out of usage and has nothing to do with clothing. It was a synonym for what we now call 'national': the same federal rules, conditions and laws for all Australians, wherever they lived. Although the constitution only specified uniform electoral laws for the Senate, the assumption was that the electoral laws for the House of Representatives would also be uniform.

The constitution could have taken a quite different tack and let the new parliament be elected according to the different franchise laws of the various states, as still happens in the United States, but it chose not to. The new parliament for the new nation would be elected on its own franchise and would run its own elections. The Commonwealth was being established as a sovereign polity, with its own parliament, responsible to its own citizens. Both houses would derive their authority directly from the people. The states would have no hand in it.

Australia's constitution placed two more restrictions on the management of federal elections. First, each voter had only one vote for each house (sections 8 and 30). There would be no plural voting, whereby people can vote in every electoral district in which they own property. Plural voting gave the wealthy propertied more say than the rest and survived well into the twentieth century for elections to the state upper houses, and is still the case for most local council elections; but it was banished from the Commonwealth.[2]

The second restriction was section 41, which prevented the new Commonwealth from disenfranchising anyone who already had the right to vote in state elections and was included to make sure that South Australians did not vote against federation.

The first election for the new nation's parliament was held at the end of March 1901, after a short campaign. All states shared the secret Australian ballot and there would be no plural voting, but otherwise their electoral systems differed markedly, creating a patchwork quilt of laws and regulations. Only in South and Western Australia could women vote. Aborigines could vote on the same basis as other citizens in South Australia and Tasmania, and with restrictions in the other states. South Australia, Western Australia and Victoria allowed postal voting. South Australia and Tasmania were treated as one electorate for elections to both houses, but in the other states members of the lower house were elected from single-member districts, as they are today. In South Australia voters put a cross in the square box next to the name of their preferred candidate; in the other states they employed the old, slow method of crossing out the ones they did not want. Most used first-past-the-post, but Queensland had optional preferential voting, and Tasmania had its complicated preferential Hare-Clark system which few non-Tasmanians have ever fully understood.[3]

Co-ordination was in the hands of Australia's first federal public servant, Robert Garran, who was appointed permanent secretary of the attorney-general's department. His first job, on 1 January 1901, was to write out longhand the first number of the *Commonwealth Gazette* and take it to the printer. His next was to arrange the first nationwide election:

> Nowadays, for a federal election we have a Commonwealth Electoral Act, complete with Chief Electoral Officer and staff, and all runs on oiled wheels. But to lay an egg a hen is needed. We could not have a Commonwealth Electoral Act till parliament was in being. All we had was a very sketchy provision in the Constitution, declaring little more than that for the first election the State electoral laws should be applied 'as nearly as practicable' and we had six willing, but puzzled, State Electoral Officers telegraphing for advice.

With the ministers all off electioneering, young Garran, then only thirty-three, was left 'to answer all questions in the name of his minister, and to run the show'.[4]

It was the state electoral officers, though, who made the arrangements for election day or—as it turned out—days, for in this first election Australians did not all vote on the same day. Queenslanders and South Australians went to the polls on Saturday, 30 March, while the other states voted the day before. In Menindee, in far-western New South Wales, the poll was postponed because some documents had not arrived, and parts of Queensland did not vote until April because of floods. Polling-booth hours also varied, closing at 6 p.m. in New South Wales and an hour later in Victoria, causing considerable confusion in the towns along the Murray.

People voted in schools, mechanics institutes, shops and outdoors in parks, though not in pubs in either South Australia or New South Wales, where legislation prohibited it. Turnout averaged 60 per cent, though it was much lower in Western Australia, which had come late and somewhat reluctantly to federation. It would not have joined a federated Australia without the influx of t'othersiders to the goldfields. In Fremantle a mere 30 per cent of registered voters bothered to have their say.[5]

Three party groupings contested the elections. Of the seventy-five seats, the Liberal Protectionists, led by Barton and Deakin, won thirty-one; the Free Traders, led by George Reid, won twenty-eight; Labor, fourteen; and independents, two. The outcome was a shock for the established colonial politicians. The parliament was directly chosen by the people, but the election had not delivered a government with a clear majority on the floor of the lower house. Labor, which had only begun standing candidates for elections in the early 1890s, would hold the balance of power. George Reid's Free Traders had done better in the Senate, winning seventeen seats to the Liberal Protectionists' eleven. Labor, with eight, would hold the balance of power there too.

The Labor caucus elected Chris Watson from New South Wales as its leader in the House of Representatives.

Barton remained prime minister, with Labor's support on supply and confidence, but he faced a tough job passing the new nation's foundation legislation. The established colonial parties were much looser than the tightly disciplined parties we are used to, and individual parliamentarians were more independent and open to crossing the floor. Labor imposed much greater discipline on its parliamentarians. It was offering Barton support for now, but there were no guarantees it would last, and it didn't. The next ten years were unstable and sometimes chaotic, as the three parties vied for control. There were seven changes of prime minister until Labor won the election of 1910 and became Australia's first majority government.

In the long hiatus between the swearing-in of the first government on 1 January and the first meeting of the new parliament on 9 May 1901, the two bills which would govern elections were drafted: one to specify who could vote, and the other to establish the electoral machinery and the voting method. Both were introduced as early as possible, on 5 June, along with a swathe of other urgent bills needed to set the new nation in motion: Immigration Restriction, the High Court, the Public Service, Customs, Defence, Conciliation and Arbitration. The second readings were scheduled for a week later, but the bills languished on the notice paper for the rest of the year while the tariff bill was debated: how much duty to impose on imported raisins, peel and ginger; whether to impose any at all on the breakfast necessities of tea and kerosene; and on and on, through every material substance and object then in daily use or production, with every parliamentarian determined to protect the industries in his electorate.

Eventually the government decided to bypass the legislative logjam in the House of Representatives. Early in 1902 both bills were introduced in the Senate by the Sydney barrister and government leader in the upper house, Richard O'Connor: the Electoral Bill on 24 January and the Franchise Bill on 4 April. The government did not control the Senate, and O'Connor had to deploy all his considerable tact and capacity for compromise to get the bills through this generally hostile house. They then went to the House of Representatives, where further amendments were made. In both cases, the parliament passed acts that were considerably different from the bills the government had introduced—and these acts would shape future federal elections.[6]

5

WOMEN IN, ABORIGINES OUT

THE FRANCHISE ACT of 1902 would determine who could vote, and the Electoral Act of the same year how elections would be managed, the roll constructed and votes counted. The debate on the complex Electoral Act (which ran to seventeen parts and 210 pages) was longer as parliamentarians argued over detail, but the debate on the Franchise Act—just five clauses and one and a half pages—tells us more about how our first parliament imagined the new nation. Women were made full citizens, but Australia's Aborigines were thrust out.

The franchise bill framed by Edmund Barton's government was wide and generous: all adult persons 'who are inhabitants of Australia and have resided therein for six months continuously' would have the vote. Restrictions were minimal: only those of 'unsound mind', 'attainted of treason', or facing or serving a sentence of a year or longer were excluded.

Introducing the bill in April 1902, Senator Richard O'Connor made clear the government's commitment to a uniform franchise for the new nation, rather than depending on state franchises and election laws. A New South Wales vote should not have a different value from one in South Australia. A uniform franchise is the only rational way to get 'a true record of the real opinion of Australians on all the difficult questions which will come up for settlement'.[1]

When the bill went to the House the first objection raised was by fighting Charlie McDonald, the Labor member for the vast Queensland outback electorate of Kennedy, who questioned the innocuous-looking word 'resided'. 'What constitutes residence within the Commonwealth?... It has been held in Queensland that because men live in tents they are not residents.' The Minister for Home Affairs, William Lyne, who was shepherding the legislation through the House, replied that it did not matter whether a man 'lives in a house or a hollow log, or spends all his time on horseback, so long as he remains within the Commonwealth for a period of six months'. Labor was not convinced. Members for outback electorates gave many examples of magistrates refusing to enrol people to vote who had no fixed address: men who lived in camps on the river banks, 'the awful swaggie' who had no stake in the country, men whose occupations compelled them to lead a nomadic life, bullock drivers who slept under their drays. Labor insisted that the parliament's intentions be made crystal clear to the district electoral registrars, so the clause was amended to read, 'who have lived in Australia for 6 months'. 'Reside', with its implications of a settled residence, was gone.[2]

McDonald's objection goes to the heart of the radical-democratic political culture being forged in Australia in the early twentieth century. The labour movement had worked hard to recruit scattered rural workers to the new unions like the Australian Workers' Union and it wanted to make sure no country magistrate could stop them voting.

Giving the vote to 'all adult persons', the bill enfranchised women. Although this seemed all but guaranteed by section 41 of the constitution, the parliament wanted to legislate for it. Both O'Connor and Lyne assumed this debate was already won. All the state Labor parties supported the adult franchise, as did most liberals. But still members wanted to have their say: most to assert their longstanding support for this democratic provision and extol its benefits, a few to repeat their doubts and objections.

Only benefits would flow from giving women the vote, claimed Lyne, pointing to the positive experiences in South Australia and New Zealand. Political knowledge and interest would increase, and women would bring their shrewd judgement to the characters of the male candidates. Alexander Poynton from South Australia added that, since women had gained the vote in that colony, political meetings had been less rowdy and much better conducted. By then South Australian women had in fact voted at six elections, including one to choose the delegates for the federation conventions and the two referenda on the constitution.

Despite knowing their cause was lost, opponents nevertheless repeated their well-worn arguments: that women would be degraded by being forced to associate with the vulgar world of politics; that it would deprive men of the responsibility of protecting them; that women didn't want it anyway; that, having little interest in politics, they would simply vote as their husbands told them to, which would give married men one vote more than a bachelor. The Tasmanian MP Edward Braddon objected because the female franchise would swell the conservative vote, which was just the reason that the South Australian senator John Downer supported it.[3]

One argument was specific to Australian circumstances. Far more women lived in the city than in the country, claimed the pastoralist and member for New England, William Bowie Sawers. Enfranchising women would shift the balance between city and country electorates, and disadvantage the latter. It was already a 'burning grievance' in country New South Wales that Sydney had so much representation.[4] Sawers knew he was on the losing side of this issue, but the objections of rural Australia to representation based on population numbers did not go away, and the less-populated country districts continued to agitate for special consideration.

Diehard conservatives aside, the majority of federal parliamentarians supported extending the vote to women, and this clause of the bill passed easily through both houses, with unanimous support in the Senate and eleven Noes, including pairs, in the House of Representatives, where a division was taken just before midnight on 23 April.[5]

A week after the bill received the royal assent on 12 June, a mass meeting was held at the Melbourne Town Hall to celebrate the victory and to put pressure on Victoria's Legislative Council, which was persisting in denying adult suffrage for state elections. Catherine Spence, now seventy-six, was on the platform. Rose Scott, who had led the campaign in New South Wales, sent a message; as did the leading Victorian suffragist Henrietta Dugdale, who was too weak to attend. Alfred Deakin, who was acting prime minister while Barton was overseas at the coronation of Edward VII, told the meeting that Australia now had 'the broadest franchise in the world', with 'a Parliament representing a continent…to be returned by the votes of the womanhood as well as the manhood of the country'.[6] But this was not quite accurate, for the act which had enfranchised women had also disenfranchised the continent's original inhabitants.

The disenfranchisement of Aborigines is a complicated and shameful story, but at least there was a fight. The franchise bill that Edmund Barton's government drew up was broader in scope and more liberal than the act which eventuated. The government did not want to take the vote away from Aborigines but ended up compromising to get its legislation passed. The debate shows that the racialist thinking of White Australia was not uniformly applied to the Aborigines and that some people were already thinking about Aborigines' rights within the quite different framework of their dispossession.

The bill that Richard Connor introduced did not mention race. He began his second-reading speech by rehearsing its main liberal clauses—a uniform franchise, no property qualification, and adult suffrage—and then said, 'There is only one other question which may, perhaps, be a matter of controversy, paragraph b of clause 3...[which] refers to those who are natural born or naturalised subjects of the King.' Quick as a flash, South Australia's Tom Playford interjected: 'That will enable a negro to come here from Jamaica and vote.'

To this 'offhand' comment, O'Connor pointed out that, although Western Australia and Queensland prevented Aborigines and coloured persons from voting, in the other four states 'aboriginals and coloured persons who are naturalized subjects of the King have a right to vote.' He reassured senators that the number of coloured people actually exercising this right would be small. Some already in Australia would be able to vote, but because of the Immigration Restriction Act passed the previous year their numbers would not grow. This act ensured that future immigrants to Australia would be white, and had overwhelming support across the political spectrum, but Barton's government had not applied the logic of White Australia to the rights of the Aborigines. Said O'Connor,

> In the first place, I think it will be recognised that the question of whether aboriginals should vote or not is not a matter to be seriously taken into consideration where they are settled members of the community. Where they have settled down in occupations of some kind, I fail to see why they should not be allowed to vote

> in the same way as is any other inhabitant of the country. I think that we might treat this question of the position of aboriginals under our electoral laws not only fairly, but with some generosity. Unfortunately they are a failing race. In most parts of Australia they are becoming very largely civilized, and when they are civilized they are certainly quite as well qualified to vote as are a great number of persons who already possess the franchise.

O'Connor's assumptions of a failing race and the benefits and inevitability of assimilation to our civilised ways offend contemporary views on indigenous rights and culture, but we must look at what he is saying: that an Aboriginal person's race should not determine their legal status. O'Connor's father was Irish and he was one of the few Roman Catholics in the parliament. Sectarian prejudice against Irish Catholics was rife in colonial Australia, and this no doubt gave him greater sympathy for the plight of the marginalised than had many of his Protestant colleagues. But his role should not be overstated. The bill was not the product of his views alone but of the ministry, including Alfred Deakin, Edmond Barton and William Lyne.

Defending Aborigines' right to vote, O'Connor also pointed out that section 41 of the constitution guaranteed the right of those already on a state electoral roll to have their name placed on the Commonwealth electoral roll.[7] The franchise laws of the colonies differed widely in regard to Aborigines. As British citizens, Aboriginal men could vote in New South Wales, Tasmania and Victoria, although Tasmania believed it no longer had any. In South Australia both Aboriginal men and women could vote. In New South Wales and Victoria, however, anyone receiving charitable aid from the government was barred from voting, which included Aborigines living on missions, as well as people in institutions for the destitute. Queensland and Western Australia specifically excluded Aborigines from enrolling to vote unless they met certain property qualifications, which few did.[8]

This combination of restrictions meant that very few Aborigines in fact voted in colonial Australia, but some did. In South Australia, for example, a polling place was established at the Point McLeay mission at the mouth of the Murray after parliamentarians visiting the mission were pleasantly surprised by the intelligent, well-spoken men and women they met there. In 1896, 102 were enrolled and eighty-one voted.[9] In the debate on the franchise bill, William Lyne claimed that some Aborigines in New South Wales voted and that he had seen them voting.[10]

When the Federation Convention had debated section 41, nobody mentioned Aborigines, although it would give a vote in Commonwealth elections to anyone already on their state rolls; on a wider interpretation it would give the vote to all Aborigines. They were mentioned, however, in section 127: 'In reckoning the numbers of the people of the Commonwealth, or of a State or other part of the Commonwealth, aboriginal natives shall not be counted.'

The purpose of this clause was not permanently to exclude Aborigines from the government's collection of statistics, but to exclude them from electoral calculations so that states like Queensland and Western Australia with large indigenous populations did not receive more seats than their white population warranted. Lacking exact knowledge of the numbers of Aboriginal people and assuming that few of them would vote, delegates decided that their numbers would not affect a state's quota of electorates.[11] When this section was being discussed at the conventions, South Australia's John Cockburn was reassured by both Deakin and O'Connor that it would have no effect on the voting rights of Aborigines already on the roll. Their vote was already guaranteed by section 41, he was told.[12]

O'Connor's hope that clause 3, paragraph 6 of the bill would not become a matter of controversy was dashed. Race was at the forefront of the minds of parliamentarians who had just established the legislative foundations of a White Australia with the Immigration Restriction Act and the Pacific Labourers Act, which expelled the Pacific Islanders, or Kanakas, working in North Queensland's sugar industry. Why, asked the Victorian senator James Styles, would those who advocate for a White Australia give Australia 'a piebald ballot box'?[13]

On the second day of debate in the Senate, 10 April 1902, the West Australian senator Alexander Matheson moved the crucial amendment excluding Aborigines from the franchise. It read: 'No aboriginal native of Australia, Asia, Africa or the islands of the Pacific or persons of the half-blood, shall be entitled to have their name placed on the electoral roll unless so entitled under section 41 of the Constitution.'[14]

Some senators were uneasy about excluding people who were subjects of the king elsewhere in the British empire, but not Matheson. A Harrow-educated businessman who had arrived in Kalgoorlie in 1894 and established a successful goldfields retail business, Matheson was unashamedly racist and saw no place for Aborigines in the new nation.[15] He had already made this clear the previous year when, during the debate on the governor-general's address, he had replied to the New South Wales senator James Walker's statement that 'This was a black-fellow's country before it was a white man's country' as follows:

> The honorable gentleman…fails to recognise that we have taken this country from the blacks, and made it a white man's country, and intend to keep it a white man's country, so that there is no earthly use in the honorable gentleman saying that 100 years ago this was a black man's country.

When Walker protested that there 'are still 100,000 aborigines in Australia', Matheson replied, 'We are aware of that fact, and it is very regrettable, and the only consolation we have is that they are gradually dying out.'[16]

In the debate on the franchise Matheson made clear that his objection to 'the coloured races is a racial one. To me it is a matter of indifference whether they are subjects of the King or whether they are not naturalized…As a voter none of them had any electoral rights in the country from which he came.'[17] He went on:

> Surely it is absolutely repugnant to the greater number of the people of the Commonwealth that an aboriginal man, or aboriginal lubra or gin—a horrible, dirty, degraded creature—should have the same rights, simply by virtue of being 21 years of age, that we have, after some debate today, decided to give to your wives and daughters.

He pointed to section 127 of the consitution, which excluded Aborigines from population counts, as evidence that the drafters 'never for an instance contemplated that aboriginals would have a vote'.[18]

O'Connor did try to reassure the Senate that because of the Immigration Restriction Act the number of natives from Asia, Africa and the South Pacific who qualified to vote was likely to be small; however, he showed little interest in defending them. By contrast, he fought hard to retain voting rights for Aborigines.

> I say it would be a monstrous and a savage application of this principle of a white Australia. I do not believe this committee will consent to go back upon what has been the policy of Australia ever since the white man came here.[19]

He believed that many of them would not want to vote, and that their numbers were shrinking as the race declined. Nevertheless, he reiterated, four of the six states had not excluded Aborigines from voting. When Matheson objected that most of them were living on charity and so couldn't vote anyway, O'Connor disagreed:

> It is altogether a mistake to suppose that the aboriginal of Australia is to be classed in every State as being a person supplied by the Government with a blanket. No doubt a great number in all the States are aided by the Government, but many of them are earning their living as ordinary members of the community...As we have in the past been liberal and jealous for those decaying races that owned this continent, and as at no time any harm or wrong has resulted from that liberality, surely we are not going to apply this doctrine to a white Australia, not only with irregularity but with a savagery which is quite unworthy of the beginnings of this federation?[20]

He pointed out that although Aborigines already on their state rolls would be able to vote,

> those very men will have to tell their sons who are becoming more civilized, and perhaps as civilized, and as worthy of the franchise as the white men among whom they are living—'Although your people owned this territory for centuries before the white man came here, although you are his equal in intelligence, it has been prescribed by the Commonwealth that you shall not have the right to vote at all.'[21]

For Matheson race was the main issue. O'Connor, however, clearly differentiated the situation of Aborigines from that of the Chinese and Indians. He claimed he was as staunch an advocate of White Australia as anyone, but for him White Australia started at the shore and was not a hard internal border; the rights of the Aborigines flowed from their prior ownership of the country.

Matheson was concerned too that giving Aborigines the vote would put power in the hands of the squatters to swell the conservative vote. He disagreed with O'Connor that few Aborigines would vote. Every squatter in Western Australia 'maintains a gang or tribe of aboriginal natives', he said. If squatters are able

> to put every one of these savages and their gins upon the federal rolls…the entire representation of that part of the country in the Federal Parliament will be swamped by aboriginal votes. Does any honorable senator suppose that these blacks will vote on anything but the instructions they receive from their masters?

These crusted-on conservatives

> never regard anything from the point of view of public policy or of the advancement of the State or the Commonwealth. They simply consider how they may put the most money into their pockets by the sale of their fleeces and their beef, and how cheaply they can get their work done.[22]

O'Connor succeeded in having 'Australia' dropped from the amendment by a majority of four and the bill, denying the vote to Aboriginal natives of Asia, Africa or the islands of the Pacific and 'persons of the half-blood', was sent down to the House of Representatives. Lyne moved that the reference to half-bloods be omitted, and that 'except the islands of New Zealand' be added, so that Maoris could vote. Maoris, with their villages, settled agriculture and capacity to organise for war, were generally regarded as more civilised than Australia's Aborigines and had been voting in New Zealand since 1867. Both these amendments were accepted.

The radical liberal lawyer Henry Bourne Higgins then moved to have 'Australia' reinserted.

> It is utterly inappropriate to grant the franchise to the aborigines, or ask them to exercise an intelligent vote. In as much as all that we are constrained to do is to keep alive existing electoral rights in pursuance of section 41 of the Constitution...I do not think that there is any constitutional obligation on the committee to provide for a uniform franchise for the aborigines.[23]

For Higgins, the ideal voter was a well-informed, independent citizen living in a civilised community. This ideal later informed his famous Harvester Judgment, which he delivered in 1907 as president of the Commonwealth Court of Conciliation and Arbitration. He based his determination of a fair and reasonable wage on 'the normal needs of the average employee regarded as a human being living in a civilized community'. Intelligence, independence, civilisation: these were what qualified a person to vote, and Higgins could see none of these qualities in Aborigines, though it is doubtful that he knew any.[24]

Labor's leader, Chris Watson, said he had 'no objection in principle to an aboriginal, who, having qualified for the franchise takes an interest in electoral matters, exercising the vote on his own initiative'. But he feared Aboriginal votes being controlled by squatters. Labor was convinced that employers would try to direct the votes of their workers if given the chance. Watson worried that in the remote districts of Western Australia and Queensland, where there were more Aborigines than whites, 'uncivilised blacks' who are 'practically slaves' of the squatters would have no chance of resisting and might 'turn the tide of an election in the interests of those who had a fair amount of money'.[25]

One Labor member, James Ronald, was troubled by excluding Aborigines as a class. Couldn't there be an education test, he asked, to make provision for 'aboriginals who may rise above their "birth's invidious bar"'? Ronald was a Presbyterian minister and so more sensitive to the claims of a universal humanity: 'To draw a colour line, and say that because a man's face is black he therefore is not able to understand the principles of civilisation, is misanthropic, inhumane and unchristian.'[26] Ronald's suggestion got no support. When Higgins's amendment restoring the original wording and excluding Aborigines was put to the vote, it wasn't even close: twenty-seven Ayes to five Noes.[27]

The five Noes were James Ronald, Hugh Mahon, Billy Hughes, Vaiben Louis Solomon and Henry Willis. The first three were members of the Labor Party, and Solomon, a long-time Northern Territorian, was close to Labor. He was also Jewish, which may have made him more sympathetic to the claims of racial minorities. Willis was a Free Trader and member for the New South Wales seat of Robertson. All were strong, vocal supporters of White Australia, but like O'Connor they distinguished between racially discriminatory immigration laws and laws for Aborigines. Alfred Deakin was not in the chamber and did not cast a vote. He had other things on his mind that day, as he had just written to Barton resigning from the ministry over a proposed increase in the salaries of members of parliament.[28]

When the bill went back to the Senate, with the word 'Australia' disenfranchising Aborigines reinserted, O'Connor reluctantly bowed to the inevitable.

> I took a very strong view that an aboriginal ought to be allowed to have his vote, and the committee agreed to that view. But the other House has taken the opposite view, and inserted the word 'Australia' for the reason that, while in New South Wales, Victoria, and other States there are a large number of aboriginals who may be very well intrusted with the franchise which they possess, in Western Australia there are a large number who, living in a state of semi-civilization in the neighbourhood of towns, might become registered, and that the clause applies not only to the blackfellows, but also to their gins. The prospect of our giving the franchise to the

half-wild gins living with their tribe seems to have startled some of our friends in the other House…Although I admit that some strong reasons were given for differentiating the case of Western Australia, I would very much prefer the Bill to be carried in the form in which it left the Senate. But, like honorable senators, the Government have to consider whether it is worthwhile to throw over the Bill because we cannot get what we want in this clause. It appears to me that, inasmuch as legislation cannot take place unless we come to an agreement, it is not worthwhile, for the sake of this particular provision, to stand out for our own way, and so run the risk of losing the Bill.[29]

In both houses, arguments against enfranchising Aborigines were a mixture of political calculation and racism. Dreadful things were said about ignorant savages, as some parliamentarians shuddered to think that the vote they had just given to their wives and daughters would be shared with such creatures. Sexual relations between white men and Aboriginal women on the frontier and in outback towns, though well known, was too shameful to be discussed, but this knowledge surely animated the horror some members felt about giving the vote to 'dirty degraded gins'. Also widely known but not openly discussed was the violence of the moving frontier in the north and the west.[30] It is striking that the attack on the government's intention to enfranchise Aborigines was led by men from Queensland and Western Australia.

Matheson had referred to some of this indirectly during the debate in reply to the governor-general's speech, when staking the claim to Australia as 'a white man's country'. In Western Australia, he said, 'very large portions of the very best pastoral country in that State are almost barred from pastoral occupation on account of the savageness of the blacks.'[31] No doubt he was referring in part to the guerrilla campaign of resistance that the Bunuba man Jandamarra, or Pigeon as he was known to Europeans, had waged in the Kimberley region for three years in the 1890s.

Similarly, the Northern Territory had been rife with violence since at least the 1880s, when a massive pastoral boom began. The Gulf Country and Barkly Tableland were settled rapidly and violently, with little regard for the rights or welfare of the people living there and with numerous punitive expeditions to teach the 'wild blacks' a lesson when they speared cattle or killed a white drover. Senator John Downer certainly knew of the violence in the north. He was premier of South Australia during the 1880s and 1890s, when the worst violence was occurring, and complicit in ensuring that there were no successful prosecutions against its perpetrators.[32]

As I read the parliamentary debates over the franchise bill, and the disgraceful comments made by so many politicians about the 'wild blacks' and their degraded gins, I wondered what was in the minds of these men as they spoke and voted. Some city-based men like O'Connor and Higgins had little knowledge of the realities of the frontier. Otherwise O'Connor could not have claimed that governments had been 'liberal' in their treatment of the 'decaying races' and had done no harm. Others, like Forrest and Downer, knew only too well that O'Connor was wrong. Matheson, who moved the initial amendment, must have smiled at his naivety. Did these men oppose giving the vote to Aborigines out of barely acknowledged shame, or even fear that this little chink of recognition of Aboriginal people's claims to equality would expose the criminal violence of the frontier? If the relatives of those killed could vote, perhaps they might take courage to speak about what they knew and had seen.

Today the disenfranchisement of Aborigines by the 1902 Franchise Act is one of the infamous stepping stones of cruelty and shame in our treatment of indigenous Australians. At the time it was barely noticed, as suffragists around the country celebrated the enfranchisement of women.

The voting rights of Aborigines now depended on how section 41 would be interpreted in relation to those states that did allow Aborigines to vote. The narrowest interpretation was that it only applied to people who were already on the state rolls; the widest, that the right could be acquired at any time under a state law passed at any time. Those already on the state rolls in South Australia, New South Wales and Victoria in 1902 could not be deprived of their vote, but what of those who turned twenty-one after that date, or who, already qualified, sought to enrol for the first time?

Parliamentary debate could not resolve a matter of constitutional interpretation, yet in the absence of a High Court judgment public servants needed to know who to enrol. Robert Garran, secretary of the attorney-general's department, advised them to take the narrower interpretation, which they did. Only those Aborigines already on a state roll could vote in Commonwealth elections.

The act did not exclude 'persons of the half-blood', and in 1905 Garran advised Queensland's Chief Protector of Aborigines that 'half-castes' were not disqualified from the Commonwealth franchise, 'but that all persons in whom the aboriginal blood preponderates are disqualified'. Garran subsequently clarified the preponderance of aboriginal blood as meaning 'ancestry'.[33] It was a simple dichotomy which rejected pressure for more elaborated racial hierarchies, with quadroons and octaroons. It should have enfranchised many more people than it did, but it was left to electoral officers to decide whether an individual was 'full blood' and ineligible, or 'half-blood' or less, and so eligible. They did so largely on the basis of skin colour and their own judgements about individual Aboriginal people's capacities.

As the states adopted joint electoral rolls during the 1920s, the Commonwealth's narrower franchise, based on Western Australia's and Queensland's exclusionary voting laws, came to prevail. As well, the new joint electoral form did not alert Aboriginal people to their right to vote in Commonwealth elections if they were already on the state rolls in 1902, thereby wrongly implying that *no* Aborigines could vote for the Commonwealth. Individual Aborigines who had been on the Commonwealth roll since 1902 because they were already on a state roll found their eligibility questioned. In 1933 eleven Aborigines living at Point McLeay in South Australia who had been voting since 1902 were disenfranchised by electoral officers. This was clearly unlawful, but the individuals concerned did not challenge the decisions. It was an arbitrary and unjust system which was not seriously contested until the 1940s.[34]

In 1924 an Indian and British subject who had enrolled in Victoria, Mitta Bullosh, challenged the Commonwealth in the Court of Petty Sessions over its refusal to add him to the electoral roll, and the magistrate found in his favour. The federal government initiated an appeal to the High Court, but quickly came under pressure from London. The British government had never liked Australia's Immigration Restriction Act, which banned some British subjects from migrating to Australia because of the colour of their skin, but it had reluctantly agreed to allow Australia to set its own rules on migration. Indians had complained loudly about this race-based discrimination. Asking the High Court to block Indian voting rights would inflame already difficult imperial relations, so, at London's request, the government dropped the case.

Then, in order to prevent Mitta Bullosh becoming a precedent for a broad interpretation of section 41, which would have extended the franchise to Aborigines and to many other excluded people in New South Wales, Victoria and South Australia, the government passed a special law to give voting rights to Indians. The 2,300 Indians in Australia were appeased, and the narrow interpretation of section 41 continued to guide the decisions of electoral officers. Had an Aborigine on one of the state electoral rolls mounted a similar challenge, Aborigines might have gained the federal franchise forty years earlier than actually happened, but none did. Nor were there any progressive lawyers offering to support them.[35]

In one respect non-Europeans were in a far better position than the Aborigines, if they had managed to slip through the immigration restrictions or had been here since the nineteenth century. Even though they were ineligible to vote if born in Asia, Africa or the Pacific (except New Zealand), their children born in Australia were eligible. In 1912, Garran wrote that 'persons of Asiatic race (for example) born in Australia are not disqualified.' For non-Europeans, it was only the first generation who were disqualified, but for Aborigines who were all born here, the disqualification passed from parent to child.[36]

Aborigines did not start to receive Commonwealth voting rights until World War Two, when those in the armed services were temporarily enfranchised. Initially this lasted only for six months after the war ended, but then all Aborigines who had served or were serving in the defence forces were given the vote for Commonwealth elections. In 1949 the Commonwealth franchise was extended to Aborigines on the state rolls, something which would have happened in 1902 had the broader interpretation of section 41 prevailed. Commonwealth electoral officers, however, made little effort to inform people of their new eligibility and did not enforce either compulsory enrolment or voting in the states where Aborigines were entitled to be on the roll. South Australia's Chief Electoral Officer, for example, took no action to enrol people who were 'primitive, illiterate, nomadic, [or] periodically nomadic'.

In Western Australia, Queensland and the Northern Territory, where most Aborigines lived, they were not on the state rolls and so still unable to vote in federal elections unless they had served in the armed forces. As well, many who would have been eligible to vote under the Commonwealth's 'preponderant blood' rule were not on the federal rolls. Some few more could vote in the Northern Territory if they were not classified as wards of the state and in Western Australia if they held certificates of citizenship, but these required them to have adopted 'civilised' manners and habits and dissolved their tribal associations. Unsurprisingly, many were reluctant to do this, and when the Select Committee established in 1961 by the House of Representatives visited Western Australia it found a good deal of ambivalence among indigenous people about voting rights.[37]

Official definitions of 'aboriginality' differed in the different jurisdictions, and for different government entitlements. Many lighter-skinned people may well have passed the 'preponderant blood' test but either did not know this and no one disabused them; or they refused to subject themselves to its offensive assimilationist assumptions. Aboriginal people identified themselves as Aboriginal on the basis of their descent and community membership, not the colour of their skin.

The 1961 Select Committee to enquire into the Aboriginal franchise found that around thirty thousand Aborigines and Torres Strait Islanders in Queensland and Western Australia were denied the federal vote because they were not on the state rolls. It also revealed 'a virtual conspiracy of silence' by the Commonwealth's electoral officers about Aboriginal and Torres Strait Islander peoples' existing voting entitlements. The Select Committee received various submissions arguing that Aboriginal people's voting rights should be tied to various tests, such as literacy, financial status or receipt of public assistance. Such criteria were not applied to non-Aboriginal voters, so the committee rejected them and recommended that 'the right to vote in Commonwealth elections be accorded to all Aboriginal and Torres Strait Islander subjects of the Queen, of voting age, permanently residing within the limits of the Commonwealth'. This was done in 1962. Registration was not made compulsory, because this would subject Aboriginal people who did not vote to fines, but voting by those enrolled was. Labor objected to voluntary registration, as this was a backward step for Aborigines in Victoria, New South Wales and South Australia.[38]

Aboriginal people did not become subject to exactly the same voting laws as other Australians until 1983, when the Hawke Labor government made both enrolment and voting compulsory for indigenous Australians.[39] Finally, eighty-one years later, Australia had the uniform adult franchise that O'Connor and the Barton government had proposed.

6

ADMINISTERING ELECTIONS IMPARTIALLY

IN JUNE 1901 the Minister for Home Affairs, William Lyne, convened a meeting of electoral officers from the different states to advise him on the federal electoral machinery. William Boothby was there. He was seventy-one and had run every election in South Australia since his appointment in 1856, proudly boasting that none had ever been tainted by bribery or corruption.[1] Lyne was especially anxious to hear how Queensland and Western Australia managed elections in their vast inland electorates. The report of these experts largely set the parameters for the lengthy and detailed Electoral Bill introduced by O'Connor in January 1902.[2]

The electoral officers considered leaving the states to run federal elections according to their differing state rules, but in the end they recommended against it. At this nation-building moment there was strong commitment to uniformity in federal matters. Although the states would continue to run their own elections in their own various ways, an Australian citizen, wherever they lived, should vote for the Australian government according to the same rules and regulations.

First, they adopted the organisational model Boothby had developed for South Australia and applied it to the nation, with a Chief Electoral Officer for the Commonwealth, a Commonwealth electoral officer for each state and a district returning officer for each division. All would be permanent, salaried public servants with their duties defined by law and set out in detailed printed instructions. This independent electoral administration charged with the impartial management of elections would be the Electoral Branch, located in the Department of Home Affairs.[3] Extra help would be needed at election times, which would for the most part come from postal officers.

The political scientist Colin Hughes calls this system, established at the outset of federation, 'the bureaucratic model', evidence of what his fellow political scientist Alan Davies called Australia's 'talent for bureaucracy'. Not only does it impose order and regularity, but more importantly it sought to keep the management of elections out of the reach of politicians.[4]

The existing state rolls varied in their completeness and purity (a pure roll was one in which there was no duplication and no dead), and only in South Australia were women on the roll. So the Commonwealth needed to construct a new federal electoral roll almost from scratch in time for the election due at the end of 1903. Again, William Boothby led the way, recommending the South Australian practices he had introduced in the 1850s. Instead of voters registering to vote annually, or just before an election, their enrolment would be continuous; instead of the onus being on the voter to apply to register, the government would conduct enrolment drives, with police, postmen and local council clerks delivering forms to every residence.

So in 1903 the Commonwealth embarked on a mammoth house-to-house census-like canvas, conducted by police and postmen on foot and horseback. People still had to fill out and return their forms, but they were delivered to their doorstep. The result was an electoral roll with the names, addresses, gender and occupations of 1.9 million people, almost double the size of the roll for the 1901 election, which was just short of a million.[5] This was around 95 per cent of the eligible population, an epic achievement and the most comprehensive electoral roll of any nation at the time. The new Electoral Branch was rightly proud.[6]

Australia's enrolment methods were a major break with British precedent. In the United Kingdom enrolment is still annual. Each year forms to be signed and returned are sent to the voter's last registered address. One can also re-register online, but the onus is on voters if they want to be able to exercise their right to vote. Pity the homeless, those who shift about, or the merely disorganised. Electoral authorities facilitate the participation of those who want to vote, but leave it largely up to them.

The other major break with British precedent was in the construction of a centralised electoral roll for the polity as a whole, in this case the new nation, with the government taking responsibility for its construction. At the time, in Britain electoral rolls were compiled by local councils, which is still the case today.

The existence of separate state and federal rolls, though, was confusing for Australian voters, and in 1905 provisions were made for the states and the Commonwealth to have joint rolls. Tasmania was the first to accept, in 1908, and New South Wales, Victoria and South Australia all adopted joint rolls in the 1920s, although Western Australia delayed until 1989 and Queensland until 1991. Today, when an Australian enrols to vote or changes their electoral details, they only have to do it once.

Australian governments have continued to shoulder much of the responsibility for enrolling voters and keeping the roll up-to-date. Until recently regular house-to-house reviews were conducted, to locate potential new voters and to monitor people's movements between electorates. In 1999 a new system was introduced, Continuous Roll Update. Information from other government agencies, such as the motor-registration boards and Centrelink, was matched with the roll to identify individuals who had changed address. These were then sent an enrolment form to confirm their new details. But the voter still had to return the form, and rates of return were disappointing.

In 2012, following a legal challenge from GetUp, Julia Gillard's government changed the legislation to make it even easier for the voter.[7] The Australian Electoral Commission could now enrol a voter directly, or change their address based on information from other government agencies. Although the AEC website admonishes the voter that 'It is still your responsibility to enrol and to keep your enrolment details up-to-date', those who just turn up at the polling booth on the day will most likely be on the roll and able to vote.[8]

In July 1903 William Boothby died. He had just completed his recommendation to William Lyne on the division of South Australia into seven federal electorates. The 1902 Electoral Act gave the power to draw electoral boundaries to the state electoral offices. Community of interest, physical features, means of communication and the existing boundaries of electoral divisions were all considered, and Boothby drew the boundaries with his usual meticulous care.[9] To honour his life's work, one of these electorates was named after him. Bureaucrats are rarely remembered for their contribution to public affairs, but every federal election night Boothby's name is on commentators' lips, even if few now know of the man's achievements.

Since the early 1970s Labor governments have further enhanced the independence of Australia's electoral administration. In 1973 the Whitlam government established the Australian Electoral Office as a statutory authority. The office was still implicitly responsible to a minister but at greater distance. In 1984 the Hawke government established the AEC under the non-ministerial direction of three commissioners, and gave it the power to manage electoral boundaries and redistributions. The Fraser Liberal government had already, in 1977, introduced regular reviews of electoral boundaries.

Politicians always take a keen interest in electoral boundaries, and if given the chance many will try to manipulate them to their advantage. In 1902 electorates were to have equal numbers of constituents, with an allowable margin of 20 per cent, and parliament retained the power to accept or reject the recommendations of state electoral offices, though not to amend them. If rejected, the redistribution lapsed and whatever population shift it was designed to remedy continued to distort the electoral boundaries.

The allowable tolerance in the size of electorates considerably advantaged rural electorates. In horse-and-buggy days this was justified by the local member's need to serve constituents scattered over large areas. A country vote was worth up to 40 per cent more than a city vote: so much for one-vote-one-value. It also greatly advantaged the Country Party and disadvantaged Labor. In 1974, long after cars and light planes had replaced horses, the Whitlam government reduced the allowable tolerance to 10 per cent. The rule was weakened by the Fraser government before being reintroduced by the Hawke government in 1984.

The Hawke government, when it established the AEC, also established the Joint Select Committee on Electoral Reform, now called the Joint Standing Committee on Electoral Matters (JSCEM), to advise the government on electoral issues. It conducts regular public inquiries after each election, and has been able to create bipartisan support for various technical improvements in the way elections are run, though its members do not always agree.[10]

Australia's commitment to uniformity in federal elections, combined with our non-partisan electoral administration, helps us to understand another of our differences from the United States, where the individual states retain broad powers over electoral administration, and whose undemocratic electoral practices shock many non-Americans.

The United States constitution explicitly left the determination of voting rights to the states and this led to big differences among the states in who could vote. Four states deprive a convicted felon of their voting rights for life, which disproportionately affects African-Americans; others only while in prison or on parole; and in two states one can vote even if in prison for murder. The American Civil Liberties Union estimates that this patchwork of state laws prevents around 5.85 million people from voting and that widespread confusion about their voting rights in effect disenfranchises many more.[11]

In the United States the determination of voting rights by individual states is combined with a highly decentralised system of electoral administration. An observer of the 2004 presidential election estimated that there were in fact thirteen thousand elections, each run by independent quasi-sovereign counties and municipalities.[12] For the most part these elections are overseen by people who are themselves elected and have strong partisan allegiances. There is thus plenty of scope for interfering with the process for partisan advantage: losing registration forms or postal votes, not providing enough polling booths in remote locations or in areas populated by supporters of the other side, malfunctioning voting machines, poorly designed ballot papers which challenge the less literate, and gerrymandering—electoral boundaries like pieces of jigsaw, with boundaries twisting and turning to take in certain areas and avoid others.

In 1965, in response to the civil-rights movement, the American federal government passed the Voting Rights Act which prohibited racial discrimination in voting rights and regulations. In 2013 this act was effectively gutted by a Supreme Court decision which allowed states with a history of racial discrimination to change voting requirements without the approval of the federal Department of Justice. Since then, Republicans have engaged actively in suppressing voters who are more likely to vote Democrat, mainly African-American and Hispanic people, but also the poor and the young.[13] Generally the reason given is prevention of voter fraud, and with neither registration nor voting compulsory the opportunities for minor requirements to frustrate voting are boundless.

Consider just two examples from the run-up to the 2018 midterm elections. In Georgia, the Republican state governor, himself standing for re-election, invoked the exact-match law to suspend voter registration applications with minor spelling mistakes, such as missing a hyphen. Seventy per cent of those suspended were African-Americans, though they are only thirty per cent of the state's voting population.[14]

In North Dakota a new state law required identification documents for voter registration to include a street address. This was a problem for many of the state's Native Americans who live on reservations and use post-office boxes for their mail because the postal service requires them to. This obstacle can be got around, but it is an obstacle nevertheless, and it mostly affects Native Americans—who have historically voted Democrat.[15]

Florida's hanging chads in the 2000 presidential contest between George W. Bush and Al Gore drew the world's attention to the small way differences in local voting requirements in the United States can affect political outcomes. Florida has twenty-five votes in the electoral college that decide the president. In some counties voters indicated their preferences by punching a hole in the ballot paper, and if the 'chad' was not punched cleanly away it was rejected. A drawn-out and complex legal challenge followed, but in the end Bush won Florida by a mere 537 votes, and world history was changed.[16] The old saying 'For the sake of a nail the shoe was lost, for the sake of a shoe the horse was lost, for the sake of a horse the battle was lost' had a new application. For the sake of Florida's hanging chads, the world lost a leader who understood the grave risk climate change poses to our collective future and who would have worked towards effective international responses.

The substitution of 'lived' for the apparently innocuous 'resided' in the 1902 Franchise Act showed Labor's sensitivity to anything that smacked of old-world property qualifications. It could not do away entirely with the need for an address for the electoral roll, but it could ensure that people working away from home for long periods could vote.

In 1902, when the electoral officers met, postal voting was already available in Western Australia, South Australia and Victoria, and they recommended that it be adopted for the Commonwealth. It was expensive to provide polling booths in every small settlement in thinly populated areas. With postal voting available, far fewer polling booths, polling clerks and other officers would be needed and costs would be greatly reduced.[17] Lyne included provision for postal voting in the bill, based on the South Australian and Victorian legislation, but he also extended the types of officers who could witness postal votes, and allowed voters, on filling in a declaration, to vote at any polling booth in their electoral district, not just the one at which they were registered.

Lyne told parliament that he was endeavouring to make the Electoral Act 'the freest, most liberal and democratic measure' ever considered by any parliament. Labor wasn't satisfied. It wanted people to be able to vote at any polling booth in the Commonwealth. Labor leader Chris Watson said that the provisions for postal voting did not meet his party's concerns. Postal services to many districts were infrequent, making it difficult for people to respond to last-minute circumstances which took them away from home. Other Labor members spoke of the itinerant workers, the carriers, drovers, shearers, miners and bush workers who did not always know where they would be on election day as they followed work across the country. Absentee voters would still have to fill out a declaration, however, if fraud were to be prevented. Labor's Charlie McDonald, who had challenged the meaning of the word 'reside' at the outset of the debate on the Franchise Bill, pointed out that many of these workers were not accustomed to writing, and would have difficulty filling out a form of any description.[18]

In the debate on postal and absentee voting, the politicians were juggling a number of desirable outcomes: encouraging as many people as possible to vote; protecting the secrecy of the ballot; keeping costs under control by limiting the number of polling booths and printing costs for duplicate rolls; enabling the poll to be declared promptly, without having to wait for votes to come in from all across the state; and preventing fraud. In the end the act provided for postal voting, and, in a compromise Labor accepted, allowed electors to vote at any state polling booth. The regulations made provision for illiterate and sight-impaired voters to be assisted with their forms.[19] In this, Australia was, and still is, far, far ahead of the democratic pack.

In the United Kingdom one is registered at the polling booth closest to one's home and required to vote there. Sometimes called precinct voting, this is a hangover from the days of a limited franchise and open voting, when members of the local community could challenge the eligibility of voters. One can apply for a postal vote, either as a one-off or permanently, or arrange for a proxy to vote, but the onus is on voters to enable their own votes, as it was for them to register in the first place.[20] Again the mobile and disorganised are disadvantaged.

Nor is any allowance made for last-minute disruptions or changes of plan. Someone working in London but living in Brighton must make sure they get home in time to vote. At the 2010 British general election some polling stations experienced a late rush and many people missed out on voting because they failed to cross the threshold before 10 p.m. Even though they had been queuing patiently, they were turned away. Authorities said they were mainly students reluctant to leave the pub, but perhaps they were voters whose trains home were delayed, a not uncommon occurrence on British Rail.[21]

In Ireland, too, voters are registered to particular polling booths. Voters may apply to be registered as a postal voter but they must give a reason, such as suffering a chronic illness or physical disability, studying at a distant institution, or having an occupation which takes them away from home on the weekday election day. They can also apply to be a special voter if they live in residential care. Otherwise it is back to the local school or community hall on the day if they want to exercise their franchise.[22] And too bad if they are working overseas, as many Irish people do. They will have to come home if they want to vote. In the Irish referenda on legalising same-sex marriage in 2015 and abortion in 2018, thousands did just that, responding to a #HomeToVote campaign, and flooding through the airports and ferry terminals before fanning out to their local booths.[23]

Canada requires people to vote in their electoral district, but anyone can vote in advance on three specified days without giving a reason, or apply for a 'special' postal ballot if they expect to be outside their electoral district on polling day. This flexibility dates to the 1990s. Prior to 1920, when Australians already had access to a range of voting methods and locations, only those Canadians who were in their local area on the appointed day and able to get to their registered polling station could vote. In 1920 three-day advance voting was introduced reluctantly for specified occupational groups such as sailors and commercial travellers, and incremental changes slowly followed.[24]

In the United States, as always, the states differ. Most allow for early voting; some allow unconditional absentee voting, and others only with reasons. Three states conduct all major elections by postal vote only.[25] Only New Zealand, among English-speaking countries, makes it as easy to vote as does Australia.[26]

Legislation and regulations making it harder or easier for people to vote embody different ideas about responsible citizenship. Among the English-speaking countries, Australia's flexibility on where we vote is as distinctive as our compulsory voting, and as revealing of our historic commitment to elections being decided by majorities of voters. Registering a person to one particular booth near where they live projects a voter with a settled residence and a settled life, a locally based elector with a job close to home. Even without overt property qualifications, the rule advantages the home owner over the renter, the long-term resident over the mobile and newly arrived, the steady and stable over the itinerant. Honouring the demand for democracy with a wide franchise, it nonetheless tilts the electoral system back to the propertied.[27]

Sometimes Australia's commitment to flexible voting arrangements is explained by our compulsory voting. If the government forces you to vote, it has to make voting easily available. But in fact this flexibility was already there in the Commonwealth's 1902 Electoral Act, and is the result of the same deep streams in Australia's political culture: our untroubled reliance on the state to organise things for us, our commitment to majoritarian democracy, and Labor's sensitivity to any voting regulation that carried the shadow of a property qualification.

7

COUNTING THE VOTE

THE 1902 COMMONWEALTH Electoral Act also established how votes would be counted in federal elections. Catherine Spence and other supporters of proportional representation had made sure that methods of counting the vote were on the political agenda, criticising first-past-the-post both for its failure to represent minorities and for creating the possibility that a candidate with minority support might win. The government's first Electoral Bill included preferential voting for the House of Representatives. It was a modified version of the optional preferential vote already used in Queensland and would, Richard O'Connor told the Senate, 'bring out in the most certain way possible the choice of the majority of the electorate'. For the Senate, the government proposed a single transferable vote, similar to Tasmania's Hare-Clark system, then still sometimes called the Hare-Spence system.

But, as with its Franchise Bill, the government could not get this bill through the parliament and the act which eventuated included neither. Instead the 1902 Electoral Act established a first-past-the-post voting system for the House of Representatives and block voting for the Senate, which is effectively first-past-the-post for multi-member electorates.

Introducing the bill, O'Connor argued passionately for proportional representation in the Senate. It was, he said, 'the true and only principle of real representation'. Like Spence, he was attracted to the pluralism promised by proportional representation. Every shade of opinion which can command a quota would be represented, he said, whereas 'throughout the British Empire for years and years phases of thought in social and political movements have had absolutely no representation whatever in the Legislatures.' It would be a credit to the Commonwealth if it could carry out 'this experiment in democracy on the largest scale', bringing into effect what has been for years 'the wishes of the most advanced political thinkers'.[1]

The government had based the bill on advice from Edward Nanson, the Cambridge-educated professor of mathematics at the University of Melbourne. Nanson too was a convert to the ideas of Thomas Hare and a frequent public advocate of proportional representation, in the newspaper, on the lecture platform and in pamphlets. In 1900 he had persuaded three leading Victorian Liberals, George Turner, Alfred Deakin and Robert Best, to incorporate his ideas into the bill which would govern Victoria's election of its first federal representatives. Although this was far too radical for Victoria's parliament, it provided the basis for the Commonwealth bill. A description by Nanson of the Victorian bill shows the similarities, down to the eight-page appendix with complicated examples of how the votes would be counted.[2] With so many new bills to draft, it seems the new federal attorney-general, Deakin, simply repurposed the Victorian bill.

These 'perfectly bewildering' eight pages of mathematical schedules and explanation were seized on by the government's opponents in the Senate. It would be quite impossible to explain to constituents, complained the South Australian Josiah Symons. Others described it as a 'mathematical maze', calculus instead of arithmetic. The system Nanson devised was far too complicated as he sought to give every vote equal weight in determining the results. He had modified the Hare-Clark scheme by including the 'Droop quota', devised in 1868 by another English mathematician, Henry Droop, and the 'Gregory method' of transferring surpluses, invented in 1880 by a Tasmanian mathematician, J. B. Gregory.[3] This Hare-Clark-Droop-Gregory-Nanson system for the election of senators was almost impossible to follow and ripe for ridicule.

In trying to provide space for minority views within a basically majoritarian system, advocates of proportional representation paid little attention to the problems of governing. As a South Australian, Symons had been lobbied by Spence for years on the benefits of 'effective voting' and had counter-arguments at the ready. Perhaps if parliament were only a consultative body it would be acceptable to overturn six hundred years of British practice that the majority of voices should elect the representatives, he said, but proportional representation threatened the possibility of workable government. It would encourage every body of 'faddists' to secure just the quota they needed to get a representative into parliament, and the big parties would be split up. Somewhat forlornly, and displaying considerable political naivety, O'Connor remarked that 'the faddists of today are the reformers of tomorrow'.[4] But faddists can come from both sides of politics, and can block reforms as much as enable them.

When the Senate sent the Electoral Bill down to the House of Representatives, preferential voting was still in place for the House, but the method for Senate elections had been amended to a block vote, much to the relief of William Lyne, whose job it was to shepherd the legislation through the House. He was glad, he said, not to have to explain the Hare-Spence system of voting, because he found it difficult to understand himself. The requirement for electors to vote for the full number of candidates in Senate elections did come in for some opposition. Why should one be forced to vote for a man one opposes? However, it narrowly survived.

Initially Labor did not have a fixed position on voting methods and gave its senators a free vote, but by the time the bill reached the House it had decided to oppose preferential voting. This 'fancy method of voting' was too confusing, said Chris Watson, compared with the 'simple and easily understood' system of placing a cross against the name of the desired candidate. Labor was no doubt worried that its less literate supporters might unwittingly vote informal, but Lyne was in no mind to defend the clause. He had just done some experimenting with preference flows and found that it was possible for the third-ranked candidate to leapfrog to victory via preferences. He amended the clause to require just a simple cross on the ballot paper.[5]

Those arguing in 1902 for preferential- and proportional-voting methods wanted to counter the increasing power of party organisation and give some room to voters to express their individual views. Those supporting simple majority-vote rules feared the disintegration of the established parties of Protectionists and Free Traders into factions, and wanted to maintain a firm two-party structure for election contests. But neither foresaw the disruption coming with the rise of Labor, which emerged as a political force in the 1890s. According to the political scientist Bruce Graham, 'Had the Barton government correctly estimated Labor's potential strength and realised that the Protectionists would definitely remain a centre party, they might not have abandoned the preferential voting proposal so lightly.'[6]

At the first federal election in 1901, Labor polled only 18.7 per cent of the House of Representatives vote. It won fourteen seats in the

House and was the smallest party after the Liberal Protectionists, which formed government with thirty-one seats, and the Free Traders, with twenty-eight. But Labor's electoral support was rising rapidly. At the 1903 election it polled 30.67 per cent of the vote and won twenty-three seats, taking five from the Liberal Protectionists, three from the Free Traders and one from an independent. The House was divided into three almost equal teams: Labor, twenty-three; the Liberal Protectionists, twenty-six; and the Free Traders, twenty-five. Alfred Deakin was prime minister and leader of the Liberal Protectionists when the election was held, and Labor agreed to support his government on confidence.

What kind of game of cricket could they play, Deakin famously asked, if they had three elevens instead of two?[7] One would have to give way. The question was which. Although Labor had supported Deakin's government after the 1903 election, it did not support all its legislation and in April 1904, much to Labor's surprise, Deakin took one withholding of support as a matter of confidence and resigned. Labor formed a government which lasted four months, which was then followed by a government led by the Free Trader George Reid, which lasted eleven, after which Deakin was back as prime minister.

In this complex dance of shifting alliances, Deakin's Liberal Protectionists were the centre party. Between Labor on the left and the conservative Free Traders on the right, they had most to gain from preferential voting as voters on both left and right would prefer them to each other. As it was, they were being squeezed from both sides, especially by Labor in inner-city seats. Deakin pleaded with Labor to grant electoral immunity to sitting Liberal Protectionists, but Labor was having none of it. These were the very seats it had most chance of winning.

So he changed his approach. In May 1906, with an election due at the end of the year, Deakin sounded out Chris Watson. Compulsory preferential voting, he wrote to him, would prevent our candidates doing so much harm to each other—and one of them would win in several Reidite Free Trade constituencies. 'It would be a great safety valve for us both? What do you think?'[8]

Again Labor was not interested. Better organised than its rivals, it had most to gain from first-past-the-post. Its tight preselections ensured only one official Labor candidate on the ballot, whereas the non-Labor vote was not only split between two parties, but non-Labor independents were a constant hazard. Labor could win seats with a minority of the vote as the non-Labor vote spread out across a field of rivals.

Nevertheless, and without Labor's support, in August 1906 Deakin's Minister for Home Affairs, Littleton Groom, introduced a Preferential Ballot Bill, which would, he said, ensure that the laws enacted by the parliament would 'truly reflect the views of the majority of the electors'. As George Reid pointed out, it was very similar to the proposal the parliament had rejected in 1902, and it was being introduced far too close to an election for voters to be educated about a new method. It could only lead to confusion and error.[9] Supported by neither left nor right, the government let the bill lapse.

At the election held in December, Labor again increased its share of the vote, to 36.34 per cent, and won three more seats. The Liberal Protectionists lost ten, including four to Independent Protectionists, who thought Deakin was far too close to Labor. It is not fanciful to argue that if the first federal government had succeeded in introducing preferential voting for the House of Representatives in either 1902 or 1906, the course of Australia's political history might well have been different. Labor's electoral rise might have been slowed, and the Liberal Protectionists might have consolidated their position as a centrist governing party. The method of voting is only one of the factors determining the formation and survival of political parties, but it is a powerful one.

FACTS ABOUT THE BALLOT.
"LOOK ON THIS PICTURE"

"ENGLISH" open voting for the Imperial Parliament.

"AND ON THIS!"

Mode of Election in the Australian Colonies, styled by the opponents of the Ballot "UN-ENGLISH."

Beverley election. Part of a pictorial broadside, issued at the time by the Ballot Society advocating the secret ballot. This was one of the two issues to which Trollope in his autobiography professed himself hostile at the election.

Ballot Society broadside, England, mid-nineteenth century.

Clockwise from top left: Catherine Helen Spence, c. 1910; Mary Lee, c. 1890; Henry Chapman, c. 1865; William Boothby, c. 1900.

Above: 'But I may not be trusted with a vote,' Melbourne, 1900.

Left: Advertisement, *Adelaide Observer*, page 3, 28 May 1898.

Waiting for election results outside the *Courier* building, Brisbane, 1907.

Left to right: Chief Electoral Officer R. C. (Ryton Campbell) Oldham; Senator Herbert Payne, c. 1920; Senator Richard O'Connor, c. 1900.

Australian soldiers voting at Etajima, Hiroshima Bay, Japan, 1946.

Country voting, ACT, 1960s.

Absentee Voting, Sydney Town Hall, 1966.

Third edition of
the playscript.

National Tally Room, Canberra, 1969.

Bondi, 1966.

Darwin, 1960s.

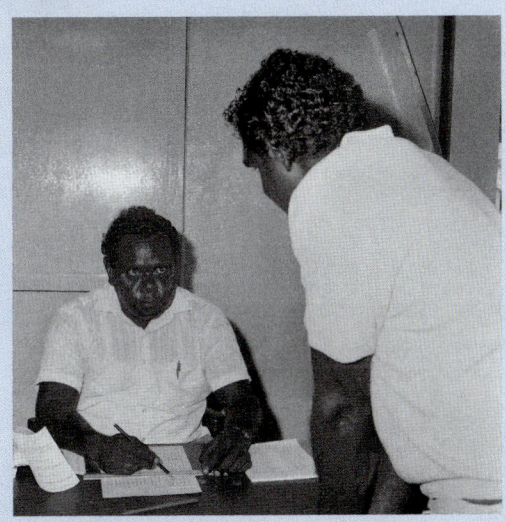

Davis, Antarctica, 2016.

Victorian state election, Footscray City Primary School, 2018.

Sausage stall and signage, Victorian state election, Merri Creek Primary School, Fitzroy North, 2018.

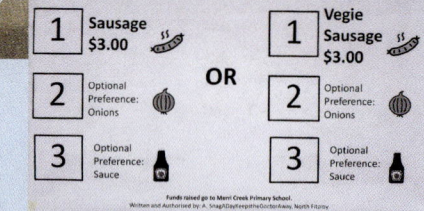

Rainbow-painted safety bollards, Southbank, Melbourne, 2018.

It was not to be. In 1909 the Liberal Protectionists and the old Free Trader Party, now calling itself Anti-Socialist, joined together to form the first federal Liberal Party and present a united anti-Labor front at the 1910 election. Much to their shock, instead of the Liberals winning comfortably as they'd expected, Labor won 49.97 per cent of the vote and formed Australia's first majority federal government.

8

EARLY ARGUMENTS OVER COMPULSORY VOTING

THE IDEA OF compulsory voting made its first appearance in Australia in a South Australian newspaper article in 1861 as a solution to unexpected consequences of the reforming Australian ballot. Election days had become dull affairs. Paper nominations and private voting booths, together with the requirement that polling places be at least a hundred yards from the nearest pub, had quietened the clamour of the hustings. With no cheering, no fights and no treating, fewer turned out. Compulsory voting was suggested as a remedy. Its second appearance was in Tasmania eighteen months later, when the solicitor-general proposed that anyone who didn't exercise their franchise should lose it, a conservative proposal that would have rapidly disenfranchised the mobile and indolent.[1]

By its third appearance, in Victoria in 1876, compulsory voting had become part of a radical electoral agenda. The government of James McCulloch was amending the colony's Electoral Act, and the

Melbourne *Herald* was urging that the act include compulsory voting as 'a practical and beneficial reform' building on the achievements of manhood suffrage and vote by ballot. It editorialised:

> The present state of affairs, as illustrated in any election contest, shows the necessity for compulsion. In few instances do more than one-half of the electors go to the poll; and in some cases only a third. And these, as a rule, are the violent partizans of one side or the other. Those who might be expected to give an impartial vote for the best man simply remain away. Of course, we expect the cry to be raised that such a provision is un-English. This is a very stale device, which, if it had any real merit or force, would have operated to check almost every serious reform this country has undertaken…We already possess a constitution that is utterly un-English since our Lords are elective; we have manhood suffrage, the ballot, and protection and they are all as un-English as they are vast improvements on the Conservative institutions of the Empire.[2]

The *Herald* also argued that every state school should be made a polling booth and that election day should be declared a public holiday. To the objection that the day would be given over to pleasure and picnicking, the *Herald* replied, 'but when a man has done his duty why should he not indulge in pleasure? A general election is usually a cause of general rejoicing.'[3]

Although some parliamentarians agreed with the *Herald*, Premier McCulloch did not and nothing came of these suggestions.[4] Twelve years later, in 1888, the Victorian government included compulsory voting in its Electoral Act 1865 Amendment Bill. The bill's main purpose was to abolish plural voting for the Legislative Assembly. Introducing the bill, Chief Secretary Alfred Deakin told the parliament that the proposal to make voting compulsory had generated a good deal of discussion. Most objections, he said, were to the imposition of penalties for failing to vote, rather than to the idea that voting should be compulsory.[5] Deakin was being somewhat disingenuous. The *Argus* reported that the Assembly had treated the idea of compulsory voting with derision: 'compelling people to vote is so ridiculous that friends of the Government marvel that sensible men could have allowed themselves to have been persuaded into proposing it.'

The *Leader* was just as scathing. It was a 'reckless', 'thoughtless' idea, 'treated with scorn in all directions'. 'Things have hardly come to pass in this colony that the citizens are to be driven to the poll by the police.' The *Leader* also pointed to a consequence which the government had clearly not thought through. The fine for failing to vote was twenty shillings, or one pound. Although there was provision for excuses, returning officers were to have extensive powers in assessing them and refusal to answer questions could lead to a month's imprisonment. Why would anyone apply for the right to vote if it exposed them to a hefty fine and possible criminal penalties? It hardly seemed like a radical plan, more like 'a cunning device of the Conservatives to assail manhood suffrage', wrote the *Leader*.[6]

The *Leader*'s response must have rattled Deakin. It was one of David Syme's stable of papers, the weekly magazine to the *Age*, which was the most influential of the colony's papers. Just a few years before, Deakin himself had been writing for both, and Syme was a mentor and friend. So he accepted defeat, characteristically suggesting that this was what was intended all along. Cabinet had placed the clause in the bill, he told the parliament, not because it expected it to be passed, but 'as an indication of what they regard as correct principle...the recognition of the obligation of every man possessed of the electoral franchise to exercise it'. Because of the difficulty of enforcing it, however, cabinet had decided to drop the clause, content that raising the issue had educated the public that possession of the vote implies an obligation to exercise it.

Deakin was a proud man, prickly about his independence, and he found much about electioneering distasteful. He fully expected, he said, that as democratic political institutions developed, some means would be found to protect candidates from the need 'to sue for favours at the hands of the electors. I say that position is not a proper one, either for the electors or the candidate...An elector should not require to be sued, and a candidate should not be called upon to sue.'[7] Deakin was objecting to candidates having to plead with people to take the trouble of voting. In 1888 political parties in the Australian colonies were weak, so much of the burden of getting out the vote fell to the candidates themselves. It was one thing for a proud man to persuade people to vote for him because of his policies or his upright and independent character; it was another to have to coax them, as if they were doing one a favour or might expect something in return; and quite another to be tempted to offer them inducements. Compulsory voting would sweep all this away.

The next attempt to introduce compulsory voting was also made in Victoria, in 1905 and again in 1906, by the conservative government of Thomas Bent. Bent was said to believe that the apathetic were more likely to vote conservative.[8] This was a common assumption. The merits of compulsory voting were also being debated in the United States, Canada and New Zealand, where some proponents saw it as a way to counter the effects of the mass suffrage by ensuring that the votes of moderate and respectable citizens would balance those of the newly enfranchised: those without property and the radical working class. In 1893 Belgium had adopted compulsory voting at the same time as adult male suffrage on just this reasoning.[9]

But no politician was going to admit in parliament that he supported a measure simply out of partisan advantage. Instead, the Victorian chief secretary, John Mackey, who introduced the bill, pointed to historical precedent among the Anglo-Saxons for whom, he claimed, voting was not a right but a duty. An appeal to the Anglo-Saxon origins of the institutions of self-government was a popular way of uniting Britain, her colonies and the United States, attributing to them a shared love of liberty, resourceful independence and restless energy. But as the United States' rejection of compulsory voting shows, Anglo-Saxon origins could suggest many paths. Mackey took them in a decidedly authoritarian direction. As it was already illegal to buy and sell votes, it followed that it should also be illegal not to vote at all: 'The State has a direct interest in seeing that a vote is cast…on public grounds alone, and not for corrupt consideration…just as the State makes rules against the corrupt voter, so it is justified…in making laws against the indifferent voter.'[10]

Notice how easily Mackey talks of the state making laws to compel the vote. This shows how little purchase social-contract and natural-rights theory had on Australians' common-sense political thinking. Mackey does not see voting as a right belonging to the individual so much as an obligation bestowed by the state. What most exercised him was the scope voluntary voting gave for small, well-organised minorities to demand that candidates pledge themselves absolutely in return for their support on polling day. This was an obvious allusion to Labor members of parliament, who were required to make a pledge to support Labor's platform and to vote in parliament as the party meeting decided, but Labor was not Mackey's main concern. It was rather the pressures applied to non-Labor candidates by well-organised total-abstinence and anti-gambling groups, often with religious backing. Mackey believed that it was voters chiefly concerned with the general public interest who stayed at home on voting day, leaving the polls to the zealots.[11]

Systematic studies of voting behaviour were more than half a century away, but Mackey's hunches were shrewd. We have seen in recent elections in the United States that the need to motivate voter turnout encourages highly targeted and divisive campaigns appealing to fear or moral outrage on issues about which a minority feel strongly, such as abortion, same-sex marriage or asylum seekers.

As happened in 1888, the Bent government's compulsory-voting bills also foundered on the problem of enforcement. With so many potential miscreants, and so many potential excuses, the legislation seemed hardly practical. And what about all the people who were not even registered?[12] Nevertheless, the Victorian bills prompted a great deal of discussion around the country, especially as there was a similar proposal afoot in Canada.[13]

Most interest groups were in favour of compulsory voting. The Farmers', Property Owners' and Producers' Association supported it, so long as every facility for voting by post was provided.[14] The *Sydney Morning Herald* gave Bent's proposed legislation a ringing endorsement. If voting were compulsory, 'we might claim that the result of an election reflected the balance of public opinion'; without it, the result 'only shows which party is the better organised' and 'we are governed by minorities'. The paper pointed out that turnout at the 1903 federal election was a mere 46.86 per cent, meaning fifty-three out of every hundred voters had not gone to the polls.[15] The *Age* agreed. Only with compulsory voting would a government represent the majority of the electorate.[16]

Sectarianism too made a contribution. In February 1909, when Victorian women were finally about to get the vote for state elections, the Protestant Defence Association worried that the Roman Catholics were already organising their women to apply for their electoral rights. The priests would then tell them how to vote. Compulsion was needed to bring Protestant women to the polls and level the field.[17]

There were a few dissenters. To the Launceston *Examiner*, the need to compel people to vote simply showed the folly of the universal franchise, which has made 'the pauper in our benevolent asylums the political equal of our wool kings and financial magnates' and given as much influence to the stupid as to the greatest thinkers.[18]

Compulsory voting made a brief federal appearance in these early years of the new century. Perhaps inspired by Victoria's attempts, in 1907 during Alfred Deakin's second government, the Tasmanian Liberal senator Henry Dobson asked his fellow Tasmanian Senator John Keating, the Minister for Home Affairs, whether the government intended to introduce compulsory voting. Keating replied that, although it was not a current intention, 'the matter may be considered at another time.'[19]

Labor parties were growing in electoral strength, supported by extensive and well-organised local and state branches and an army of members available for canvassing. By contrast, non-Labor parties had rudimentary electoral organisations, with a ramshackle array of electoral leagues and intermittent local committees and agents. Opponents of Labor concluded that its political success was the result of a superior capacity to get supporters to the polling booths, and that if voting were made compulsory non-Labor would benefit.

Some Labor men believed that with compulsory voting 'the workers would sweep the polls.'[20] Victorian Labor, on the other hand, was officially opposed because 'every property owner was on the roll by virtue of being a ratepayer, but from 50 to 70 per cent of workers were not on the rolls,' it estimated.[21] This was likely an exaggeration for the Commonwealth electoral roll, but may well have been true for the state roll. Not only were working-class men less likely to own property, but much of their work was itinerant. Some of these men had no fixed address; others were away from their place of residence for long periods, or moved frequently and didn't bother to re-register. Labor was only likely to support compulsory voting once compulsory registration removed its doubts about the bias of the rolls.

9

LABOR IN POWER

IN APRIL 1910 Labor formed Australia's first majority government and Andrew Fisher, a tall, handsome Scotsman, became prime minister. Labor had already had two short periods of government in the unstable three-cornered contest of the Commonwealth's first decade.

When Chris Watson became prime minister in 1904, he led the first national Labor government in the world. It survived a mere four months, losing office when Deakin withdrew his party's support, but it provided competent administration, proving that Labor could govern and adding another feather to Australia's cap as the world's leading democratic nation.

Labor took office again at the end of 1908, when it withdrew its support from Alfred Deakin's second government. Fisher was now the leader and the party had grown impatient with supporting Deakin. Nor would it refrain from running candidates against progressive Liberal Protectionists by granting them electoral immunity. Finally, Deakin and his party were forced to join with the New South Wales Free Traders turned Anti-Socialists in a new party to present a united front against their working-class challengers. Called first the Fusion and then the Liberal Party, it quickly sent the second Labor government packing and Deakin became prime minister for the third and last time. The second Labor government had lasted a little more than six months, and the Liberals were confident of winning the election in 1910.

This confidence was misplaced. The turnout was up, at 62.8 per cent compared with 51.48 per cent in 1906, and Labor enjoyed a 13-per-cent swing. It won just short of 50 per cent of the first-past-the-post vote and forty-three of the seventy-five seats in the House of Representatives. It also won control of the Senate.

Australia's first prime minister to control both the House and the Senate was not one of the liberal lawyers who made the federation, but a self-taught man who began his working life as a boy of ten in the coal pits of Ayrshire and was already experienced in working-class politics when he arrived in Queensland in the mid-1880s. Andrew Fisher settled in Gympie, where he worked in mining and joined in the fast-emerging labour politics. In 1893 he was one of sixteen Labor men elected to Queensland's Legislative Assembly, and in the first federal election he was elected as the member for Wide Bay. Now he was leader of the young nation.

At the end of the new government's first full year in office, in December 1911, the Minister for Home Affairs, King O'Malley, introduced its electoral legislation with a flamboyant flourish: 'an Electoral Bill is the very embodiment of the might and majesty of the political life and organization of a nation...An honest ballot is the breath that fills the lungs of the Commonwealth. An honest election is the blood that circulates through the veins of the Commonwealth.'[1] Tall and bearded, with flowing tawny hair, O'Malley was cut from a different cloth to Labor's miners and rural workers. He was an insurance salesman with a gift for self-promotion who had emigrated from the United States.

He claimed to have been born in Canada, as only British subjects were eligible for parliamentary office in Australia.[2]

Labor had the numbers in the House and the Senate to make this bill into law, and it greatly strengthened Australia's already distinctive democratic electoral traditions. The changes were wide-ranging. The government abolished postal voting, extended provisions for absentee voting, introduced Saturday polling days, and required political parties to report their campaign spending and newspapers their revenue from political advertising. It also, on the advice of the Chief Electoral Officer, introduced compulsory registration of voters.

The most contentious change, and the one closest to Labor's heart, was the abolition of postal voting while making absentee voting even easier than it already was. In 1902 Labor had argued for electors to be able to vote anywhere in the Commonwealth, but had compromised on the more limited option of being able to vote anywhere in the elector's state. Now they could accommodate the needs of their nomad workers, who could write the name of their preferred candidate on a blank piece of paper in any polling booth in the country and, even if it was incorrectly spelt, it would be a formal vote. Provision was also made for people to vote early, in the presence of any Commonwealth electoral registrar, a reform of great benefit to seamen, who were often away for weeks at a time and likely to vote Labor.[3]

The Opposition pointed out that these changes to absentee voting would especially benefit Labor voters, as indeed they were intended to, but the main force of its ire was directed at Labor's abolition of postal voting. Labor believed that postal voting was being abused by their opponents, that the free and secret ballot was being compromised. It argued that rich householders were pressuring their domestic servants and squatters their workers to apply for postal votes, and were then monitoring their votes.

Medical men, who were authorised to witness postal votes, came in for particular suspicion. James Fenton, the Labor member for Maribyrnong, claimed that on the last election day a doctor had used a motorcar to collect twenty votes which were handed to the returning officer. Despite not arriving by post, they were still counted. Another medical man had told Fenton that he had received a circular from a certain city office which read:

> On polling day there will be under your care a large number who may not be able to vote by attending a polling booth. Enclosed you will find a number of application forms for postal ballot-papers. Will you kindly see that they are distributed among your patients, and see also that they get postal ballot-papers and vote.

This the medical man did, telling Fenton, 'I witnessed their votes, and saw that they voted all right.'[4]

Furious Liberals believed that the abolition of postal voting had less to do with protecting the secrecy of the ballot than with disenfranchising their supporters. One said Labor's Electoral Bill should be called 'The Liberal Disenfranchisement Bill'; another claimed it 'bristled with many sinister and suspicious aspects'.[5] Arrangements were in place for people to vote early or cast absentee votes, but both required visiting a polling booth or an electoral office. Over and again Liberal parliamentarians railed at the disenfranchisement of the housebound sick and elderly, and those who lived in the backblocks far from any polling booth. Did they expect a man to walk ten or fifteen miles just to vote?

Then there were the new and expectant mothers. Heavily pregnant women did not appear in public, and women who had just given birth rested at home for a number of weeks. The New South Wales Liberal senator James Walker calculated that since a woman is compelled to stay at home for about one-eighth of the year preceding and following the birth of a child, of the roughly 120,000 women who give birth each year, one-eighth or fifteen thousand of them would be disenfranchised.[6]

The Liberal member for Bendigo, John Quick, read out a resolution from the Australian Women's National League, which had been formed the previous year in Victoria to safeguard the interests of the home, women and children: 'That this Council, representing many thousands of women, enters the strongest possible protest against the action of the Federal Government in proposing to disenfranchise thousands of women throughout Australia by the abolition of the postal vote.'[7] The AWNL was right. Women had been the majority of the thirty thousand postal voters at the 1910 election and would bear the brunt of its abolition.[8]

Labor's disregard for the voting rights of those confined to their homes reveals the limitations of its masculinist worker-focussed politics. Labor's paradigmatic voter was the unionised male worker, and it made sure he could vote wherever he was. The abolition of postal voting was a blatant act of disenfranchisement and Liberals were right to oppose it. Eventually Labor would have to give way. But whatever the calculations both sides were making to gain a political advantage, there was also a clear ideological difference, with Labor's class-based emphasis on the economic conflicts of the workplace marginalising home- and family-based political issues of particular relevance to women. Robert Menzies would later make much of Liberals' support for the home in his 1942 radio broadcast to the Forgotten People. Until the Whitlam government embraced second-wave feminism thirty years later, women voters favoured the Liberals.[9]

Labor also made voter registration compulsory. This policy innovation was based on the advice of the Chief Electoral Officer, Ryton Campbell Oldham, another of the unknown heroes to whom we owe our democratic electoral system. Oldham was a strong advocate of compulsion in electoral matters, chiefly on grounds of administrative efficiency. He had a bureaucrat's pride in his systems; he and his officers were building a card index 'to secure a clean and continuously effective roll which will, at all times, be free from duplications'. Under the current system of voluntary enrolment, he argued, there were too many errors and omissions 'due to public neglect, carelessness, and apathy', with many people believing that 'it is the duty of the electoral administration to follow them from place to place, and relieve them of the obligation of taking action in the preservation of their electoral rights.' Australia's exceptionally large migratory population, with at least 20 per cent of city electors changing address each year, placed an unreasonable burden on government officers responsible for the roll, he said. 'It should be the duty of all qualified persons to enrol within a (reasonable) prescribed period, and to transfer or change their enrolment when they remove from place to place.'[10]

Labor had no problem with compulsory enrolment. After all, it supported compulsory unionism, and the pledge compelled Labor parliamentarians to accept majority-endorsed Labor policies. Caucus accepted Oldham's recommendation, and O'Malley suggested to the parliament that this was the first step towards compulsory voting in a society where the government already visited a good deal of compulsion on its citizens.

> There is no doubt that, in time, if the people grow gradually to realize the necessity, they will decide to have compulsory voting; but at present we are taking the first instalment. There is compulsory registration of births and deaths without objection, and compulsory vaccination in regard to which we only occasionally hear any protest. There is compulsory military service throughout the Commonwealth with very few objections; and also compulsory census and statistical returns by individuals. There is compulsory registration of persons practising professions, or following certain

businesses; and there is compulsory education in every State of the Union. We have compulsory notification of infectious diseases, and we are compelled to comply with the requirements of Sewerage Boards, as anybody who owns property in Melbourne knows full well. How, then, under these circumstances, can anyone object to compulsory enrolment?[11]

Indeed, few in the parliament did, except to ask why the government wouldn't go the whole way and introduce compulsory voting. George Fuller, who had been Minister for Home Affairs in Deakin's third and last government, said it was a necessary corollary of compulsory enrolment: 'if we are to have the one we ought certainly to have the other. The object is to get not only as full and complete a roll, but as full and complete a poll of the electors as possible.'[12] Numerous other members of the Opposition parties also said that they would support compulsory enrolment if it was accompanied by compulsory voting, including Alfred Deakin and the New South Wales Free Trader Joseph Cook, who would become Opposition leader when Deakin retired in January 1913. Why would so much official effort be expended on getting people onto the rolls if there was no outcome?

The legislation was introduced in the Senate by Labor's George Pearce, who argued that the right to vote is a duty as well as a privilege; and that as Australians had not had to fight hard to wrench the right to vote from a reluctant government, it was even more a matter of duty. At first glance this is an odd argument, but it reveals just how statist or top-down Australians' conception of citizenship was and how easily it sat with government compulsion. Australians viewed citizenship as a status conferred on them by the government. Like O'Malley, Pearce pointed to all the other areas of life in which Australians now accepted compulsion: education, vaccination, military training. Apart from a few hardline Liberals from New South Wales, no one saw anything objectionable in the state compelling its citizens to register.

Why didn't Labor also commit to compulsory voting in 1911? Perhaps, as the Hobart *Mercury* explained, it was because they knew it would 'bring to the polls those voters of the Liberal Party whose indifference at the present time is really the only reason that the Labor Party is in power'.[13] This was an explanation to comfort Liberals after the shock defeat in 1910, but it also expressed the view that compulsory voting would moderate the impact of working-class political organisations.

In the absence of modern survey techniques, no one really knew whether this view had any merit. The chief reason Liberals supported compulsory voting was that it would oblige Labor to drop its opposition to postal voting. It could hardly make voting compulsory and then not enable the housebound to vote. Although the caucus had in fact accepted a report on compulsory voting when the bill was being prepared, Labor's opposition to postal voting was stronger than its support for compulsory voting.[14]

The bill contained another contentious proposal: that candidates disclose their election expenses and newspapers report the amount spent on election advertising. This brought to the surface deep-seated mutual suspicions the Labor and the Liberal parties held of each other's organisational resources, which continue to this day. The Liberals relied on paid canvassers during election campaigns, whose wages would be an obvious expense, while the wages of union officials, state Labor members, and senators not facing re-election would not register. They would be out in force campaigning with their free rail passes. The West Australian Liberal John Forrest complained that in the last election 'an army of union officials and state and federal Labor members overran the constituencies, working in the interests of Labor candidates.' His side could not have organisation without paying for it.[15]

Even without the support of the trade unions, the Labor Party had a far more unified organisation than the Liberals, and was much more successful in mobilising volunteers. But Labor knew that the money power backed the Liberals, together with the main daily newspapers whose editorials could be expected to support them. As well, Liberals would have more cars to use in canvassing and to transport voters to the polls. Not so, said Cook:

> motor cars were sent from Sydney to Parramatta to help the Labour candidate, who had one of his own to assist him throughout the election campaign, whilst I was chasing him with a pony and sulky. One of the main qualifications leading to his selection to contest the seat was, I understand, that he possessed a motor.[16]

In 1911 cars were still a novelty. Elaborate, unreliable machines that only the super-rich could afford had appeared in Australia around the turn of the century, but after 1908 Henry Ford's Model T began to be assembled locally, making this amazing new form of transport more widely available, including to well-off farmers, medical men and clergy. The advantages for political campaigning were immediately obvious.

It is not clear how many cars there were in Australia in 1911: the first readily available national figures for the number of cars and trucks are for 1922. Use had grown during the war, when the number of registered motorcars and trucks was just short of one hundred thousand, about one for every forty-four people of voting age.[17] In 1911, when cars first appear in political debates about voting, there would have been a good deal fewer. Cars were so great an advantage to a party supported by the well-off that in 1918 a Labor caucus subcommittee recommended that they be eliminated from elections.[18] This proposal came to nothing.

Labor's other innovation in 1911 was so important to our electoral traditions that it deserves a chapter of its own.

10

VOTING ON SATURDAY

AUSTRALIA IS ONE of only a handful of countries to hold elections on Saturdays. Cyprus, Malta, Iceland, Latvia, Slovakia, Taiwan and New Zealand are the others. Except for New Zealand, these are not countries we often compare Australia with, and New Zealand has only been holding elections exclusively on Saturdays since 1951.[1] We've been voting on Saturdays federally since 1913, and since the end of the nineteenth century in Queensland and South Australia. Labor's federal caucus committed to Saturday voting in 1901, and made it law in its 1911 revision of the Electoral Act.[2]

Most countries go to the polls on Sundays, except in the Protestant-dominated Anglosphere, where public activities on the Sabbath other than attending church have historically been severely restricted. Continental Sundays, when people drank, shopped and made merry, were regarded by Protestants as papish defilements of the Lord's Day. In Australia, until restrictions started to be lifted in the 1980s, shops, pubs and picture theatres were all closed on Sundays, there were no sporting events, and the streets were deserted.

Canada, the United States, the United Kingdom and Ireland all vote on weekdays: Canada, Monday; the United States, Tuesday, though some states declare a public holiday; the United Kingdom, Thursday; Ireland, generally Friday. Weekday voting, without the easy absentee and postal voting Australians enjoy, makes casting a vote much more difficult for many people, particularly when they are required to vote in their electorates. New Zealand shows the benefits of voting on Saturday: even without compulsory voting, its turnouts are generally well above 75 per cent, though it does have the booster of compulsory registration.[3]

During the week most people are at work or studying or both. An American study of reasons for not voting found that the most common was the inability to get away from work or study commitments.[4] Thirty American states do guarantee people time off work to vote, in some cases even paid leave, but only if the voter doesn't have two, three or sufficient hours of their own time available, generally before or after work. This being the United States, the allotment of time varies from state to state. The other twenty states make no provision at all.[5] Even when leave is available, employees still have to request it, so exercising this right assumes they feel able to ask their employers for the time off without fear of adverse consequences, and that employers won't obstruct them for partisan reasons. And it is no help at all to the casually employed, who lack the fixed hours the legislation assumes.

Canada also allows one to ask for time off to vote, if three consecutive hours are not available at either end of the working day. The situation there and in the United States is better than in the United Kingdom, where there is no legislation at all to allow voters to take time off to vote. People do have the right to request it, but their employer is not obliged to grant it. For the 2017 British election the #TimeToVote campaign encouraged businesses to give their employees the time to get to the polling booths.[6]

In Australia, Saturday afternoon was a half-holiday for most workers in the late nineteenth century and for much of the twentieth. It was also the weekly shopping day for many farmers. During the debate on the Franchise Bill in 1902, the Queensland senator Thomas Glassey said that in Queensland, where people voted on Saturdays, election days were 'generally looked at as a sort of holiday'.[7] They also boosted turnout. Queensland state elections in the early twentieth century were consistently above 70 per cent, and often into the eighties.[8]

Despite the likelihood that holding elections on Saturdays would get more voters to the polls, the Opposition objected when Labor included it in its 1911 Electoral Bill. A Victorian Liberal, John Quick, said that 'it will disfranchise all belonging to the Hebrew faith and the Seventh-Day Adventists, who regard Saturday as the Sabbath, and will not engage in secular occupations on that day.' The conservative Australian Women's National League also objected, and Quick read into Hansard its resolution that Saturday voting be reconsidered, as it 'disenfranchises large sections of the community to whom this day is sacred'.

Seventh-day Adventists were not a great cause for concern, as they generally held themselves aloof from the inevitable and often grubby compromises of politics and didn't vote anyway. Labor members from both Queensland and South Australia pointed out that Jews had managed to vote on Saturdays in their states, and there had been no protests. In fact, Labor proposed to extend polling hours until 8 p.m., to allow Jews to vote after the Sabbath ended at sunset. As elections were usually held in April, May or June, this was thought to give them plenty of time. They would, though, responded Quick, 'be debarred from acting on the committees of candidates, pressing electors to go to the poll, and doing other electioneering work'.[9] Quick failed to mention the many more working people who were freed for electioneering by

Saturday voting, perhaps because the businessmen and home-based women who made up the bulk of non-Labor's volunteers were less constrained by employment obligations than were Labor's workers.

The Opposition also raised practical, administrative concerns. Because of the later closing of the poll, counting would have to continue into Sunday, when telegraphic, transport and postal services were virtually suspended, and everyone would have to wait longer for the result. These objections were slight, motivated more by partisanship than anything else. This is particularly so of the AWNL, as Saturday voting was to prove of enormous benefit to women. Many women were still a little coy about entering a polling place alone, and would now be able to go with their menfolk. The less shy could leave their husbands to mind the children while they slipped out to vote.

Labor's bill passed, and the 1913 election was held under the new arrangements on Saturday, 31 May. This was the first Commonwealth election held after a government had run its full term, and the first since registration had been made compulsory. The roll grew by more than half a million, but turnout also increased, from 62.80 per cent in 1910 to 73.49 per cent. In South Australia it went from 55.33 to 79.87 per cent. Making it compulsory to register seems to have impressed on voters' minds the importance of fulfilling their civic duty.[10]

The *Age* described the scenes at the Melbourne booths, where cars were much in evidence to ferry people through the wet and windy streets. The Liberals had the largest number of vehicles, but Labor too was well supplied, and 'in the camaraderie of the election fight as often as not a Labor voter would travel in a Liberal car and vice versa.' The wild weather made this first Saturday vote a test of its citizens' patriotism, but the *Age* concluded they rose to the challenge and that the atmosphere in the larger booths was like a huge bazaar, with eager canvassers, crowds of onlookers, busy officials, lines of voters and tired mothers with their infants resting on the benches at the end of the hall. Crowds were generally cheerful, but at every polling booth there were moving scenes as an invalid or cripple was lifted, carried or wheeled into the booth, some even arriving in ambulances.[11]

If Labor hoped that Saturday voting or the abolition of postal voting would give the party a decisive advantage, it was wrong. The turnout may have been considerably higher, but Joseph Cook and the Liberals won the election by a single seat. After providing the Speaker, they had to rely on his casting vote to maintain the confidence of the House; and Labor still controlled the Senate.

Almost immediately, Cook decided to seek a double-dissolution election, hoping to improve his government's majority, so he introduced bills he knew the Labor-controlled Senate would reject. One of these was an Electoral Bill which restored postal voting and abolished Saturday voting.[12] The minister in charge was Willie Kelly, the handsome member for Wentworth with a fondness for practical jokes and a languid Eton drawl. The repeal of Saturday voting was, he said, on the advice of the Chief Electoral Officer for administrative convenience, despite, as Labor pointed out, this being the day on which electors had most time for voting.[13]

In the debate over restoring the postal vote, Kelly produced figures which supported the claim that Labor opposed postal voting because it advantaged the Liberals. Of the eighty-four thousand postal votes cast in the 1910 election, forty-nine thousand had been for the Liberals and thirty-three thousand for Labor.[14] This figure was considerably higher than the twenty-nine thousand postal votes claimed during the debate on the 1911 legislation. But the actual number was not the issue so much as Labor's belief that postal voting was open to abuse in ways that disadvantaged it. So Labor dug in. Andrew Fisher claimed that in Queensland a justice of the peace, when authorising postal votes, had effectively said to the wives and daughters of employers, 'your bread and butter depends on the way you vote.' Some, he claimed, even provided blotting paper to the voters to detect the name of the preferred candidate. Fisher continued:

> Honorable members will notice how eager Ministers are to have voting done away from the polling booths. How eager they are to get as many persons as possible to vote in their own homes, surrounded by Liberal and influential ladies and gentlemen willing to assist in the process of voting. The Democratic principle always has been that voting should be done at the ballot-box, in the presence of responsible officials, and of the scrutineers of the candidates, not behind the scenes, where influence can be brought to bear.[15]

Labor refused to pass the legislation in the Senate. By the middle of 1914 Cook had the trigger in place to request a double-dissolution election. In the event, the trigger pulled was not the failure to pass the Electoral Bill, but legislation which prohibited the government from giving preference to union members for employment. This was the Commonwealth's first double-dissolution election. It resolved the deadlock, but not in the way Cook had hoped.

After a mere fifteen months of government, the Liberals lost office. The swing to Labor was 2.42 per cent and the number of Labor senators actually increased by two.[16] Labor was back in government and Fisher was again prime minister, but he was now leading a country at war, for between the dissolving of parliament on 30 July 1914 and the election on 5 September, King George V had declared war on Germany.

11

QUEENSLAND MAKES IT COMPULSORY

THE NEXT STEP along Australia's path to compulsory voting was taken by the Liberal government of Queensland. The Australian Workers' Union had been organising to raise the political consciousness of Queensland's itinerant rural workers: joining them up, getting them to enrol and encouraging them to vote for Labor candidates. Like Victorian Premier Tommy Bent before him, Premier Digby Denham thought that compulsory voting would benefit his side, matching the trade unions' successful mobilisation of the Labor vote with a law to compel apathetic and disenchanted Liberal supporters to the poll. Compulsory registration and compulsory voting were introduced together in late 1914, with an election due the following year. The maximum penalty for non-compliance was two pounds, a hefty penalty of more than two hundred dollars in current money.[1]

At first Queensland's Labor caucus was opposed to compulsion, but when Digby's two proposals came before the parliament they let them through, and focussed objections on the government's replacement of absent voting with postal voting, and on the state's onerous residency requirements for enrolment, which disadvantaged nomadic rural workers. The government was deeply unpopular, especially with farmers, and Labor's leader, Tom Ryan, predicted that introducing compulsory registration and voting 'would rebound upon them in a way they do not expect'.[2] Although Belgium had had compulsory voting for men since 1892, no one mentioned it. Likely they didn't know.

The election on 22 May 1915 was the first in the English-speaking world at which voting was compulsory for everyone on the electoral roll. The turnout was 88.14 per cent, a notable increase on the 70 per cent which had voted in 1912, and the female turnout was 90.09 per cent. The Brisbane *Courier* concluded that making voting compulsory had effected 'a great improvement in securing a more general expression of the will of the people'. And Ryan was right. The higher turnout did not advantage the Liberals as Denham had hoped. Instead, a swing to Labor of more than 5 per cent gave it a clear majority and Labor began an election-winning run which kept it in government in Queensland until 1929.[3]

The Queensland victory persuaded many Labor members around the country that compulsory voting might be to its advantage. When Labor's federal conference met a few weeks later it resolved to adopt it both for general elections and for referenda. Caucus, however, was not yet completely on board, and agreed only that it would be compulsory to vote in the upcoming constitutional referendum.[4] Labor was trying to extend the Commonwealth's powers over trade and commerce, corporations, industrial relations, and combinations and monopolies at the expense of the states. Similar proposals had already been put and defeated in 1911 and 1913, though support was much greater in 1913 than in 1911, falling just short of 50 per cent of the national vote. This time Labor was hopeful of success.[5]

Ominously for Labor's support for compulsory voting, the attorney-general, Billy Hughes, was a sceptic. Calling those who failed to vote 'civic idiots', he argued that compulsory voting was a poor alternative to political education: 'The driving force of the Labour movement has not been compulsion but inspiration. To force the people onto the roll is a most indifferent substitute for that enthusiasm which led many to walk sixty miles to vote.'[6]

When Fisher introduced the Referendum Bill to federal parliament in June, he foreshadowed that a Compulsory Voting Bill would be introduced to facilitate the referendum. By August, Hughes, despite his misgivings, had prepared one based on the Queensland precedent, but with a lower penalty for non-compliance of only one pound.[7]

Labor parliamentarians were not the only people arguing for compulsory voting in the middle of 1915. So too were the bureaucrats. In July the Royal Commission on Electoral Matters tabled its report. The commission had been established by the Cook Liberal government to investigate the conduct of the 1913 election, including the conduct of Labor's Minister for Home Affairs, the flamboyant King O'Malley, who had interfered 'in a most undignified manner' with the appointment of at least forty-three electoral officials in his Tasmanian electorate of Darwin (now Braddon) because he suspected they were opposed to him.

While this was and still is frequent practice in O'Malley's birthplace across the Pacific, it flouted Australia's commitment to non-partisan and professional electoral administration by permanent public servants. As key witnesses to the inquiry, electoral officers were keen to advance the case for their importance. The commission recommended defining the powers of the Chief Electoral Officer and restricting intervention by the minister. It also took a swipe at Labor's stubborn opposition to postal voting: 'The Electoral Law should not be forged as a party weapon but should aim to make it possible for every elector to record his vote.'

Around seventy-seven thousand electors had been unable to vote in 1913, 'many of whom would be mothers of our people, fulfilling the noblest duties of life'. So long as postal voting was available, the royal commission recommended 'compulsory voting as a natural corollary of compulsory registration'.[8]

The Compulsory Voting Bill was debated in September 1915. The thrilling landing on the Gallipoli Peninsula on 25 April was stalemated by the Turks defending their homeland, and casualties were mounting. Cook asked, 'When people are nursing their griefs, when 100,000 of our best voters are overseas fighting the battles of Empire, is this the time to embark on a partisan experiment?' The Opposition had a point. Compulsion was being brought in not for a general election but for a referendum on 'a purely party question'. Cook himself supported compulsory voting, and he all but offered to drop the Opposition's objection to the bill if Labor would reintroduce postal voting. It was limiting compulsion to the partisan referendum that he objected to. If compulsory voting was such a good idea, shouldn't it apply to general elections as well?

Labor could give no convincing answer to this, fuelling the Opposition's suspicion that it was using the referendum as an experiment to test the Queensland effect. Only one parliamentarian spoke up against compulsory voting as a matter of principle: George Wise, a Deakinite Liberal and now the independent member for Gippsland in Victoria, who objected to compelling the indifferent to vote. But Labor had the numbers in both chambers and the bill to make it compulsory to vote in the referendum was passed.[9]

Despite his oft-quoted promise to defend the empire to 'our last man and last shilling', Andrew Fisher was not a militarist. It was his third stint as prime minister and the strain of managing both a country at war and a restive labour movement was damaging his health. There was pressure to introduce conscription, which he opposed, and the labour movement was determined to wrest control of prices away from the war profiteers and to use a Labor government to pursue its general social and industrial policies. As well, an impatient, ambitious Billy Hughes was snapping at his heels. The strain became unbearable, and at the end of October Fisher resigned and went to London as high commissioner.

Billy Hughes was unanimously elected to succeed him. Hughes was a very different man from the calm, thoughtful Andy Fisher: short and slight to Fisher's muscular height, more brilliant and energetic, but also devious, an ambitious, pugnacious schemer compared with the straightforward Fisher. And where Fisher was a democrat both from conviction and disposition, Hughes was a temperamental authoritarian who would soon split the party to which they had both given their best adult years.

Immediately on becoming prime minister Hughes faced a concerted campaign against Labor's referendum. The Liberal Opposition, supported by business and the press, argued it was divisive when the nation should be united to fight the war. The conservative Australian Women's National League delivered a monster petition of fifty-five thousand signatures to the prime minister's office urging postponement. The premiers, four of whom were Labor, were unhappy at the prospect of losing even more state powers to the Commonwealth. Their own reform programmes would be undermined, and they feared that the centralisation of power over industrial issues could also be used for conservative ends.

The referendum proposals seemed headed for a third defeat, and Hughes decided to abandon them in exchange for an agreement from the states to transfer the relevant powers to the Commonwealth for the duration of the war. This was never likely to happen, as it would have to clear the conservative Legislative Councils in each state. Labor's left wing was furious and never forgave Hughes for this betrayal.[10] The Commonwealth's first experiment with compulsory voting was over before it began.

The following year, in October 1916, Hughes held the first of his two notorious referenda on conscription. The federal government already had the power to conscript men for military service within Australia. Hughes wanted to extend this to overseas military service. Here is the question put to the people:

> Are you in favour of the Government having, in this grave emergency, the same compulsory powers over citizens in regard to requiring their military service, for the term of this War, outside the Commonwealth, as it now has in regard to military service within the Commonwealth?

We would now call a national vote on a question other than altering the constitution a plebiscite, but at the time it was called a referendum and it was not compulsory to vote.

Soon after he became prime minister Hughes had travelled to London, where the decisions about the deployment of Australia's troops were being made. Like Australian prime ministers before him and after, he pushed his nation's claims to a voice in the management of imperial defence, and reminded the British of Australia's loyalty and the sacrifice of our bravest and best already underway. In the six months he was gone, however, Australians' enthusiasm for the war had waned, with recruitment falling as casualties mounted.

Britain had introduced conscription in January 1916 and in Australia the Liberal Opposition, most of the press and many prominent public men were all clamouring for conscription for overseas service. The labour movement was deeply divided. Many were loyal imperialists and supported Hughes's position, but not all; the movement also included pacifists, anti-militarists and, after Britain's brutal response to Ireland's Easter Uprising earlier that year, anti-imperialists. Some, like Queensland's premier, Tom Ryan, though loyal supporters of the war, opposed conscription as an unwarranted extension of government power.

Hughes pressed ahead regardless. He had no principled objection to the idea of compulsion: after all, in both trade unions and the Labor Party itself members were compelled to follow rules and abide by majority decisions. He believed that conscription was for the greater good, and, as the question reminded voters, the state already compelled some military service. When the first referendum was narrowly lost after a bitter eight-week campaign, Hughes was devastated, as were other supporters of conscription. Though the vote was voluntary, turnout was the highest ever, at 83 per cent, but the No vote was 51.2 per cent. The referendum was lost in South Australia, Queensland and New South Wales, all states with Labor governments.[11]

Almost immediately, the federal Labor caucus passed a motion of no-confidence in Hughes as its leader. Defiant, he led a group of loyalists out of the room and negotiated a coalition government with the Liberal Opposition and the formation of a new party called the Nationalists. He was still prime minister, but the party he abandoned would not win federal government again until 1929. This was the first great Labor split.

The Nationalist government led by Hughes won the election in 1917 in a landslide. With recruitment stagnant, Hughes called another referendum on the same question, to be held on 20 December 1917. This campaign was even more bitter and divisive than the first, with Melbourne's Roman Catholic archbishop, Daniel Mannix, prominent among the opponents. Again the proposal was lost, with a slight increase in the No vote to 53.79 per cent and the Liberal-governed state of Victoria joining the opponents.

Groups who might have been expected to defend civil liberties—Australia's Liberal and conservative politicians, the press and the Protestant churches—all spent two years and more arguing for the government's right to compel its citizens into military service overseas, with little regard for arguments about freedom of conscience or individual rights. During both referendum campaigns, the government wielded the War Precautions Act ruthlessly to suppress and censor the No case. The first Commonwealth security surveillance agency, the Australian Special Intelligence Bureau, intercepted the correspondence of anti-conscriptionists and raided their homes, and there was scant regard for freedom of association as the meetings and rallies of anti-conscriptionists were frustrated and raided.

'The supreme duty which a democrat owes to his country is to fight for it,' said Hughes. If individuals did not recognise this duty, then the state would compel them to perform it anyway.[12]

12

THE FARMERS GET A PARTY

GIVEN THEIR BELIEF in the freedom of the individual, Liberals were ambivalent about disciplined party organisation; it was, after all, one of their major lines of difference from Labor, with its pledge and caucus control. But the splitting of the vote in the first-past-the-post system was a real electoral problem for them. All the party could do to protect its official candidates was to ask intending rivals to refrain from standing.

By 1911 New South Wales, Tasmania, Victoria and Western Australia had adopted some form of preferential voting, and at the 1914 federal election Liberal Prime Minister Joseph Cook promised to introduce it for federal elections if his government was returned. But Cook's Liberals lost to Labor, which had no interest in changing a system which so clearly worked to its advantage.

Preferential voting did not come back onto the federal political agenda until 1918, when the Labor renegade Billy Hughes was prime minister of a Nationalist government. The Nationalists' electoral organisation was weak, and rural pressure groups, precursors of the Country Party, were impatient at the neglect of primary producers by the city-based parties. They wanted to run their own candidates.

John Hall, a founder of the Victorian Farmers' Union, issued Hughes a blunt warning: 'it is with difficulty that organisations such as ours were prevented from running candidates at the last election, when, with three candidates in the field your cause would inevitably have suffered with the split vote.' The Farmers' Union would no longer guarantee electoral immunity to the Nationalists, and had decided to run candidates at all future elections. It had seen Labor's success in getting working men into parliament; it would do the same for farmers.

This threat was made good at a by-election in Flinders in May 1918. John Hall stood, risking the defeat of the Nationalists' star recruit, Captain Stanley Melbourne Bruce, a wounded Gallipoli hero who had returned to Australia after years in England to manage his family's substantial importing business. Two days before the poll, Hall withdrew as a candidate after the government promised that it would introduce a bill for preferential voting. Six months went by but there was no bill.

Another by-election, this time in the West Australian seat of Swan in October 1918, showed the urgency. There were four candidates: one Labor and three others, including one from the Farmers' and Settlers' Association. Despite frantic cables from Nationalist leaders in the east, urging two to withdraw, none did and Labor won the seat with 34.36 per cent of the vote.[1]

When this seemed about to repeat itself in a by-election two months later for the Victorian seat of Corangamite, the government finally acted on its promise. A bill introducing preferential voting, already in process, was rushed through in time to apply to the by-election.

The South Australian Patrick Glyn introduced the bill for the government. He claimed that the purpose of preferential voting was to secure majority representation in single-seat electorates. It would also, he said, weaken the effectiveness of party preselection, as rival candidates of the same political persuasion could stand without risking a Labor victory. This would provide a remedy for party splits, as well as giving expression to wider electoral opinion.

Labor members put up a few half-hearted objections: voters would get confused between crosses for the Senate and numbers for the House, they said. And why was it necessary when there were only two candidates in most contests?

The bill, yet another overhaul of the Electoral Act, also reintroduced postal voting. Predictably, Labor complained of abuses, but its new leader, Frank Tudor, lacked intellectual and oratorical firepower; and, anyway, Labor didn't have the numbers.[2] With preferential voting in place for the by-election, Corangamite became the first federal seat to be decided by preferences. Labor's Jim Scullin, a future prime minister, topped the poll with 42.5 per cent of the vote, but the Farmers' Union Party candidate, William Gibson, won the seat with preferences from the other two non-Labor candidates to become the first farmers' representative in the federal parliament.[3]

The government then moved quickly to introduce preferential voting for Senate elections as well, to be in place for the election due at the end of 1919. Again the main argument was majority rule. Labor complained that the change was being drive by party considerations but it mounted no cogent argument against the principle of majority rule. How could it? It was the basis of its own organisation.

A small number of senators were ardent advocates of proportional representation for the Senate. Why wasn't it being introduced instead of this 'clumsy, cumbersome, complicated Bill', asked Senator Herbert Pratten, a Nationalist from New South Wales. The proposed change to a preferential system was not in fact likely to prevent the massive majorities produced by the simple block system currently in place, he pointed out, and minorities would still be unrepresented. Proportional representation, on the other hand, would increase voters' choice and loosen the major parties' stranglehold on parliamentary numbers.

Pratten believed proportional representation would 'revivify' the Senate, and make it a real house of review 'with independence of thought and action'. Another supporter of proportional representation, the Tasmanian Nationalist senator Thomas Bakhap, predicted, 'If the people of Australia find themselves face to face with a Chamber in which only one party is represented, something will break.' He knew that there was little chance of achieving proportional representation with the current government, but he believed it the duty of its advocates to keep it alive as a possibility.[4] The government, though, pressed ahead and introduced a preferential system for the Senate.

Bakhap is an interesting figure. Born to a young Irish girl in the Ballarat Benevolent Asylum, he grew up in Tasmania's Chinese community, after his mother married a Cantonese man who gave him his name and taught him Cantonese. This may have made him more sensitive to the need for minorities to be represented. Although he supported White Australia, a necessary position for anyone seeking elected office, he publicly, though erroneously, identified as being of mixed blood and championed the interests of Australian Chinese. Also important was his Tasmanian experience of the Hare-Clark system, which showed that proportional representation was 'a fair and equitable system'.[5]

At the 1919 election the government's introduction of preferential voting was well and truly vindicated by the results. The Nationalists won thirty-seven seats, the farmers' candidates eleven and a demoralised Labor Party only twenty-six. The result in the Senate confirmed Pratten's claim that little would change with the introduction of preferences and that massive unrepresentative majorities would continue. With 43 per cent of the vote, Labor won only one seat. The Nationalists, with 46 per cent, won eighteen. At the previous election, in 1917, the Nationalists had won a clean sweep and now had thirty-five out of thirty-six Senate seats.[6]

Preferential voting led to another of Australia's distinctive electoral practices: party volunteers handing out how-to-vote cards to advise people on the order of their preferences. The most dramatic change, however, was the entry of a third major party into Australian politics. In 1919 candidates from five farmers' parties had won eleven seats. These subsequently merged to form the Country Party which, in 1922, won a further three and the balance of power. It was only then that the Nationalists realised what a militant political operator they had allowed to emerge. The new Country Party would not be an easily placated rural faction within the broad Nationalist church, but a politically savvy sectional party driving hardnosed bargains.[7]

The first was its conditions for entering into a coalition government: Hughes to be replaced as prime minister by Stanley Melbourne Bruce; and five ministers in an eleven-member cabinet, including the roles of treasurer and deputy prime minister for the party's leader, Earle Page, a country doctor and newspaperman from New England. Rather than take the country to another election, Bruce agreed and the government became known as the Bruce–Page government.

Bruce was tall, with the fashionable good looks and smooth, brushed-back hair of a silent-movie star: a wealthy man who dressed in spats and plus-fours, played golf, and drove the latest-model motorcar. With the reserve and good manners of the well-bred, he could be relied on to spring no surprises, and was as different from Hughes as Fisher had been before him. Believing in the unified national interest he had served as a soldier, Bruce did everything he could to make the coalition work and resisted moves in his own party to take on their country cousins. He brought aggrieved rural interests into the centre of government. With a more combative leader, the coalition may not have survived.

As it was, the coalition agreement was outrageous. The Country Party got almost half the ministries with 12.6 per cent of the first-preference vote (the Nationalists had polled 35 per cent). But in 1922 Australia was a grieving and divided nation: sixty thousand dead, many more mentally and physically wounded, sectarianism rampant after the conscription referenda, a killer epidemic of Spanish influenza, a Labor Party struggling after its first great split. The nation-building optimism of the years after federation were like another age.

13

COMPULSORY VOTING ACHIEVED

IN 1916 THE Victorian branch of the Labor Party adopted compulsory voting for state elections. Labor was in Opposition and the premier was Alexander Peacock, a Liberal. In July of that year the member for Richmond, Ted Cotter, was given the task of putting Labor's policy into effect. Receiving the assignment, he wasted no time. In August he gave notice of his intention to introduce a private member's bill and by the end of the year it was ready, based on the provisions of the Commonwealth's 1915 Compulsory Voting Act.[1] The conservative *Argus*, not usually a supporter of Labor initiatives, commended it as deserving careful consideration. Although noting that there was a great deal to be said against the proposal, the only problem the *Argus* raised was that of enforcement, with nothing at all about the infringement of liberties.[2]

Cotter's bill was debated in the Legislative Assembly for the first time in August 1917. His major argument was that, given the positive effect in Queensland, it would improve turnout, which was even lower in state elections than federal. He noted too the wide discrepancy between the commitment of country and city voters. In country electorates around 75 per cent of voters turned out, whereas their city cousins could only manage 48 to 50 per cent.[3] At the end of that year the Victorian attorney-general, Agar Wynne, said that the government proposed to make voting at state elections compulsory.[4] Perhaps it would have, but the new Nationalist Party was deeply divided in Victoria and by March the following year a new team was in charge. Compulsory voting, though, was now on the agenda.

During the federal debate on the 1918 Electoral Bill, which restored postal voting and introduced preferential voting for the House of Representatives, Robert Menzies' uncle, Sydney Sampson, moved an amendment to include compulsory voting. Sampson was the member for the sparsely populated rural electorate of Wimmera in western Victoria. His main argument was the burden on the public-spirited of getting the indifferent to the poll: 'There are those who will not go to the poll unless they are carried, preferably in a motor car…Why should some persons in the community have the responsibility of carrying thousands to the polls?'

The amendment was not accepted by the minister responsible for the bill, but it had supporters. Frank Tudor, leading the Labor Party after Hughes's defection, agreed that the demand for motor transport was a problem. Even in city electorates like his of Yarra, 'people insist on being carried in a motor car to a booth half a mile away, not even a wagonette will do.'

Dr Maloney, who had been a member of the 1915 Royal Commission on Electoral Matters which had recommended compulsory voting, said that the majority of intelligent witnesses had supported it. He believed it had popular support and that sooner or later it would be adopted.[5]

Since 1901 the federal parliament had been meeting in Melbourne, borrowing Victoria's Parliament House for its debates while the Victorian parliament met in the Exhibition Building. This was a temporary arrangement: first until the site of the new capital had been chosen, and then until it had a parliament house and some government buildings. Federal parliament did not move to Canberra until 1927. Just as the meeting of the 1898 Constitutional Convention in Adelaide was fortuitous for women's suffrage, so the presence of federal politicians in Melbourne during this period helped the cause of compulsory voting. Every year from 1917 to 1922 Cotter reintroduced his bill. Every year he met the same stumbling block: compulsory voting presupposed compulsory registration, and this was waiting on the amalgamation of the state and Commonwealth electoral rolls.[6]

Commonwealth and state electoral officers had already recommended this, but it was proceeding slowly, state by state. The delay was further depressing the vote in state elections, as many voters did not realise that two rolls were in operation and that they had to take steps to register on each. When they turned up on state election day, they discovered they were not on the roll.

The annual debate on Cotter's bill, from 1917 until 1922, built support for compulsory voting, familiarising federal politicians with the case and demonstrating the growing community support. Each year speakers from both sides of the Victorian parliament extolled the benefits of compulsory voting, and frequent debates on the question by various political organisations were reported in the newspapers. Since first introducing the bill, said Cotter, the Nationalist, Labor and Farmers' Union parties in Victoria had all supported the principle at their annual conferences, as had the Australian Women's National League.[7]

As importantly, no strong opposition case had been articulated. Objections were ad hoc and mostly about practicalities. Few made arguments about preserving the freedom of citizens not to vote.

Very low turnouts at the 1921 and 1922 Victorian elections stimulated support for the proposition. At this time, separate elections were held for the Assembly and the Council. The turnout for the 1921 Assembly election was low enough, at 57.26 per cent, but for the Legislative Council election in May the following year it was disastrous: 13.3 per cent, a mere 46,891 of the 353,467 eligible voters.[8] The new premier, Harry Lawson, deplored the apathy. Victoria, he said, would have to adopt compulsory enrolment, a uniform roll and compulsory voting. What was wanted 'was a decision of the whole of the people and not a section of the people'.[9]

At the federal election in December 1922 the turnout was only 57.95 per cent of registered voters, a decline of 13 per cent from the 71 per cent who voted in the previous election, in 1919. In Tasmania turnout hit the shocking low of 45.93 per cent. Queensland was the highest, with 82.66, 26 per cent more than any other state.[10]

It was clear that Queensland's compulsory voting for state elections had carried over to the federal sphere, perhaps from habit, perhaps because Queenslanders didn't distinguish sufficiently between state and federal elections and thought they would be fined for not voting. Or perhaps, as advocates of compulsory voting hoped, it was because being forced to vote made people more politically aware and engaged. At the Victorian state election held on 26 June 1924, turnout was again low, 59.24, suggesting the problem was becoming chronic.[11]

Other bad habits were forming. The burden of supplying fleets of motorcars was becoming more onerous for candidates and party workers. It was worst in the country. Echoing Sydney Sampson in 1918, Albert Dunstan, the Country Party member for Eaglehawk, complained to the 1923 annual meeting of the Victorian Farmers' Union that 'a large proportion of people would not vote unless they were taken to the polls in motor cars.'[12]

A private member's bill to make voting compulsory was introduced in the Senate by the Tasmanian Nationalist Herbert Payne on 17 July 1924. Payne had a longstanding interest in electoral matters. In 1918 he had been a member of a Select Committee on the Tasmanian Electoral Act, which considered how to facilitate voting for soldiers on active service. As soldiers would have scant access to campaign material, it suggested including the candidate's party affiliation on the ballot paper.[13] This idea was finally taken up by the Hawke government in its overhaul of the Commonwealth Electoral Act in 1983. No party has yet adopted Payne's 1934 suggestion of circular ballot papers to neutralise the impact of donkey voting, although in 1979 Tasmania adopted another innovative means to achieve this end: the Robson rotation, where the order of candidates' names is randomised among ballot papers.[14]

Payne's bill was guided through the lower house by his fellow Nationalist Edward Mann, the member for Perth. Although the bill was not being put forward by the Nationalist government, Payne and Mann were confident of their party's support. At a Nationalist Party meeting just before the parliamentary debate, twelve members had spoken in support of compulsory voting and only one against. The Nationalist leader and prime minister, Stanley Melbourne Bruce, had said nothing at the meeting but indicated he would be guided by the view of the party. The new Country Party's party meeting supported it unanimously, and everybody knew it was already Labor policy.[15]

The bill was a simple one, based on the 1915 Compulsory Voting Act, and with no distracting other measures attached. The penalty for not voting was set high at two pounds, the equivalent today of $160.[16] Payne's second-reading speech started inauspiciously, with a housekeeping argument that compulsory voting would deliver better value for the considerable sums of money already spent on compulsory enrolment. But he quickly hit his stride with his key concern, that for parliament to represent the people it had to be elected by the majority of the electors, not just the majority of those who turn up to vote. It should be 'a reflex of the mind of the people'. If people show no interest in who their representatives are, then over time there will be a deterioration in the quality of the laws governing the country, he said. Majoritarian democrats, unsettled by the low federal turnout in 1922, hoped that compulsory voting would bring, in Payne's words, 'a wonderful improvement in the political knowledge of the people'.[17]

In the House of Representatives, Mann too stressed the majoritarian reasons: 'If the principles of democracy are to be properly applied, it is evident that some attempt should be made to ensure that those who govern at least represent the majority of the governed.' He did acknowledge the objection that this was an interference with the liberty of the subject, but then dismissed it, claiming, 'Individual liberty is less likely to be invaded when the legal control is that exercised by the real majority of the people.' No fear here of the tyranny of the majority.

The debate was short, with only two opposing speakers. Most time was taken up by the member for Boothby, the silvertail lawyer and pastoralist John Duncan-Hughes, who criticised the haste of the bill which prevented him from consulting his constituents on their views, as well as the likely expense of enforcement. He also complained of its interference with the individual's liberty, but spent little time elaborating on this.

In the debates in both chambers, only one speaker made sustained objections to compulsion as a matter of principle: the New South Wales Labor senator Albert Gardiner, who had been a fierce anti-conscriptionist.[18] He was troubled by 'anything in democracy which savours of compulsion', and regarded it as a 'further infringement on the liberty of the individual'. However, as a Labor member, he would abide by the party's policy.[19]

No one else raised a word in either place. After a debate of less than an hour the bill was accepted unanimously by the House of Representatives without division and it passed without amendment through all remaining stages that day.[20]

At the federal election fourteen months later, on 14 November 1925, the turnout was 91.39 per cent, an increase of more than 32 per cent on the 1922 election. Herding the uninterested and apathetic to the polls did not increase the informal vote, as some sceptics had predicted; in fact, quite the opposite. It almost halved, from 4.51 per cent to 2.36 for the House of Representatives, although it was somewhat higher for the Senate at 6.96.[21]

The effect was most marked on women's voting. Until then, according to the political scientist Finn Crisp, women's turnout was around 10 per cent less than men's. Compulsory voting closed the gap.[22]

The Nationalist–Country Party coalition won convincingly, gaining ten seats. Prime Minister Stanley Bruce was quick to see the benefit of the higher turnout. Having fought the election on extending the Crimes Act to maintain industrial law and order, he could now claim that 'our mandate has been given to us by the whole of the people.'[23]

Within three years, Victoria, New South Wales and Tasmania had all introduced compulsory voting for lower-house elections, and Western Australia followed in 1936. The conservative bastions of the state legislative councils put up a fight, but compulsory voting settled into Australian electoral practices with scarcely a murmur.

Only in South Australia, the cradle of our earliest electoral innovations, was there visible resistance. The Legislative Council, elected on a much more restricted franchise than the Assembly, kept sending the legislation back. Turnout in South Australia fluctuated between 59 and 77 per cent until 1941, when it hit a low of 50.69 per cent. The following year, compulsory voting was adopted for the lower house and the turnout shot up to 88.53. It was not compulsory to vote in Legislative Council elections in South Australia until 1985!

	Qld	Vic	NSW	Tas	WA	SA
Legislative Assembly	1915	1926	1928	1928	1936	1942
Legislative Council	Council abolished 1921	1935	1928	1928	1964	1985

Years of introduction of compulsory voting in state elections.[24]

14

THE RISE OF MINOR PARTIES AND THE SENATE

OVER THE HUNDRED years since it was adopted by the federal parliament, the system of preferential voting for the House of Representatives has had only minor tweaks. In 1984 the alphabetical listing of candidates was replaced with allocation of places by lot. Some enterprising candidates were changing their names by deed poll to surnames beginning with 'A' and 'Aa'. Also in 1984 the names of registered political parties were printed on the ballot papers, so that voters could more easily identify their preferred candidates. The effects of preferential voting, however, have changed over the last half-century or so.

Until the 1950s preferential voting for the House of Representatives fulfilled the purpose of its introduction: to allow non-Labor candidates to compete with each other without giving the seat to Labor. It created one new party, the Country Party. Since then, in conjunction with proportional representation in the Senate, it has enabled other political players to enter the electoral contest. The first was the Democratic

Labor Party (DLP), formed in 1955 when the Labor Party split over communism, followed by a parade of minor parties trying to gain political traction through the allocation of preferences: the Australia Party, the Australian Democrats, the Greens, One Nation, and a host of micro- and single-issue parties and independents. It has remained very difficult for candidates outside the major parties to win seats in the House of Representatives, although this is changing. After the 2016 election there were five representatives on the crossbench.

Since the 1990s the number of seats decided by preferences has increased markedly. Thirty-one seats went to preferences in 1983, sixty-three in 1993, eighty-seven in 2001, and in 2016 an astonishing 102 out of 150 seats. These were no longer the traditional two-horse race between Labor and the Coalition. And where preferences once helped the Coalition win seats, they now more often help Labor.[1]

By contrast, preferential block voting in the Senate was not a success. As Thomas Bakhap and others had predicted when it was introduced, in what was sometimes described as the 'windscreen-wiper effect' it produced massive, unrepresentative majorities for one side or the other, just as the simple block-voting system had done. Labor had won all contested eighteen seats in 1910 before it was introduced and won them all again in 1943 under the preferential system; non-Labor won them all in 1919, 1925 and 1934.

Preferential block voting for the Senate continued until 1948, when the Labor government of Ben Chifley replaced it with proportional representation using the single transferable vote. The trigger was the government's decision to increase the size of the House of Representatives from seventy-five to 121 seats. As the constitution required there to be approximately half the number of senators as MPs, the Senate was enlarged to sixty. The expanded Senate would make the imbalance in the parties' representation there even more obvious. Echoing Bakhap thirty years earlier, John Edwards, the clerk of the Senate, said that 'a Senate of 60 members all belonging to one party would make a farce of Parliamentary government.'[2]

So, finally, the Labor government introduced the proportional representation that had been in the Commonwealth's first Electoral Bill. The government's electoral fortunes were on the slide and Opposition Leader Robert Menzies accused Labor of trying to prevent an expected wipe-out in the Senate at the next election. This was clearly a strong motivation, but the belief that proportional representation was fairer had never gone away; nor had the argument that it restored to voters some autonomy from the major parties. The Proportional Representation Society, of which Catherine Spence was a founding member, had continued to advocate for it, as had parliamentarians like Bakhap and Senator Herbert Pratten. Almost half a century after federation, the two houses would now be elected as Australia's first government had intended.

Way back in 1919 Pratten had hoped that proportional representation would create a more representative and effective Senate. The block-voting system only ever delivered unrepresentative Senates that were more often than not rubber stamps for the government of the day. When Chifley's Labor government introduced proportional representation in 1949, however, nothing could have been further from its mind than to encourage new parties or to hand control of the Senate to independents. Yet this is what happened. Sometimes this is described as a revival of the Senate, but in fact it was a transformation.

Since 1948 the government of the day has controlled the Senate in only three periods: 1959–62, 1976–81 and 2005–07. The rest of the time the government has had to depend on the support of one or more independents or minor-party senators to pass its legislation. Sometimes, as when the DLP held the balance of power, this has been largely automatic, but since the formation of the Australian Democrats in 1977 crossbench senators have become more independent. The Australian Democrats' vote collapsed in 2004, but other minor parties have taken their place (and, in some cases, already seen their own vote collapse): the Greens, Family First, One Nation, Palmer United, Nick Xenophon's team, the Liberal Democrats, and more.

After the 2016 election—a double dissolution, which has a lower quota—the government had only thirty-one senators and the Opposition twenty-six, with a whopping nineteen on the crossbench, including nine Greens. The major parties complain that proportional representation makes it hard for governments to govern, but Australian voters have embraced the chance it gives them to balance a majoritarian party-controlled House of Representatives with a broader representation in the Senate of contemporary political positions.

The report card on the benefits of proportional representation in the Senate is mixed. The system has created minor parties like the DLP and the Australian Democrats which, in their time, represented significant minority sections of opinion, and, in the case of the Greens and One Nation, still do. But it has also encouraged a proliferation of single-issue candidates and micro-parties. Senate ballot papers, which went from a vertical to a horizontal format in 1940, have been getting longer and longer to accommodate the numbers. At the 2013 federal election the Victorian Senate ballot paper was 1.02 metres long and sight-challenged voters needed magnifying sheets to read it.[3]

Until 1983, when the federal Labor government introduced above-the-line voting, voters were required to place a number against every candidate. Rates of informal voting were high. With above-the-line voting candidates are grouped by party and voters are required only to mark their party of first preference.[4] Most did from the start, which significantly improved the formal vote, but it also meant that voters handed control of preferences over to the parties, major and minor alike. Most minor parties and independents did not secure enough votes to come within cooee of a seat, but such was the complexity of preference distribution that sometimes they did.

A very clever man, Glenn Druery, saw an opportunity. In 1996 he founded a micro-party called the Outdoor Recreation Party to contest seats in the New South Wales upper house, which had proportional representation. He realised that if the minor parties agreed to preference each other before the major parties, then they would increase the chances of at least one minor party winning a seat. Druery tried the idea out in the 1999 New South Wales elections for the upper house and the Outdoor Recreation Party won a seat with only 0.2 per cent of first-preference votes. He then took his preference-harvesting strategy to the federal arena, forming an alliance among minor parties. In 2013 the Australian Motoring Enthusiast Party hit the jackpot when its candidate, Ricky Muir, won a seat with 0.5 per cent of first preferences.[5]

The major parties were alarmed, and in 2016 the Coalition amended the electoral law to limit the scope for preference deals. Now a voter can either number at least six boxes above the line for the parties or groups of their choice, or twelve boxes below the line. No preferences are distributed beyond the voters' selections, so preferences no longer end up with an individual or party those voters find reprehensible. The intention is to starve the micro-parties while enabling parties with substantial support still to win seats.[6]

15

LIBERALS PUSH BACK

COMPULSORY VOTING BECAME normal—as Australian as voting in speedos or a bikini on the way to the beach. But in the 1980s, with the rise of the new right, as politicians began to argue for deregulation and individual choice and to attack state-provided services, compulsory voting came into range. Conservative thinkers in the Anglosphere were pushing back against both the social and cultural revolutions of the 1960s and 1970s and the big-spending state of the post-war era, arguing for traditional family and gender roles even as they argued for the winding back of government regulation and for greater individual choice in the marketplace. It was a contradictory mix. The argument for voluntary voting was part of the push to wind back government. To compel people to vote was authoritarian, an attack on individual freedom, a product of the nanny state, so the argument went. The other countries with which we compared ourselves had voluntary voting. Why shouldn't we join them?

During the 1990s some Liberals attempted to repeal compulsory voting. In 1991 and again in 1993 the Liberal Party's Federal Council passed motions calling for its repeal. In 1994 the state Liberal government of South Australia introduced legislation to end compulsory voting, which was defeated in the upper house by the combined vote of Labor and the Australian Democrats.[1] After John Howard defeated Paul Keating to become prime minister in 1996, the Joint Standing Committee on Electoral Matters recommended the introduction of voluntary voting. The numbers on the all-male committee were five Coalition, three Labor and one Democrat. It included the South Australian senator Nick Minchin and the Tasmanian senator Eric Abetz, both Liberals and long-time active opponents of compulsory voting.

Its abolition, said Minchin, was 'one of his longstanding passions'. Compulsory voting was 'an appalling form of authoritarianism' that 'corrupts democracy and…corrupts the parties'.[2] In a 1996 article for the *Parliamentarian*, the journal of the Commonwealth Parliamentary Association, he described compulsory voting as 'the most glaring departure from the principle of individual freedom in Australia'. It was, he wrote, 'a fundamental breach of the civil liberties of individuals in a liberal democracy', and 'the right not to vote is a basic freedom.'[3] Minchin tilted the tensions in liberal democracy decidedly towards the liberal, with little regard for majoritarian arguments.

Minchin's article was remarkably similar in argument and wording to the JSCEM's report, suggesting that he was the driving force in drafting it. The report cited many submissions supporting repeal, such as:

> the compulsion to attend a polling booth, on threat of financial penalty, does not reflect a free vote. The right to vote is a privilege, to be exercised after due diligence and consideration of the candidates. Should…there be no suitable candidate presenting for election, the compulsion to attend a polling booth has no democratic standing.

The report also repudiated common arguments in favour of

compulsory voting, such as that voluntary voting would undermine the legitimacy of Australian election results. This argument, it said, 'is difficult to sustain, given that virtually every other democracy in the world manages without compulsion'. If Australia is to be a 'mature democracy', compulsory voting must be abolished. The report dismissed comparisons with the low turnouts in American presidential elections, as 'there are factors at work in the United States that are unique to that country' which do not apply in Australia, nor in most Western democracies with voluntary voting.

Perhaps the strongest argument for voluntary voting, said the report, is that it would revitalise the political parties which were suffering long-term decline. 'To date the political parties have conspired to use the law to do what in virtually every other democracy the parties themselves must do—namely maximise voter turnout.' If voting were voluntary, parties would be forced to recruit members and rebuild their branch structures, in both safe and marginal seats. The report also quoted the 'former ALP pollster and campaign strategist' Rod Cameron. Compulsory voting, he said, forced parties to appeal to 'the emotions of the "lowest common denominator", people who without compulsion "would not vote in a month of Sundays"'.

Finally, the report cited British studies of voter turnouts which suggest that non-voting is essentially a function of lack of interest in the process, rather than of class or income (as if these were independent variables). 'There is no evidence from those studies to suggest that voluntary voting somehow disenfranchises the poor and underprivileged,' it claimed, flying in the face of decades of political-science research on voter activity.[4]

The three Labor members of the committee, Stephen Conroy, Laurie Ferguson and Rob McClelland, submitted a minority report. Their arguments were a little more nuanced than those made in the early twentieth century, but essentially they expressed the same majoritarian ethos. 'Compulsory voting allows the entire electorate to feel they have a degree of ownership of government decisions' and ensures that parties aspiring to govern develop policies that 'appeal to an extremely broad spectrum'. The contemporary United States showed the dangers of voluntary voting: abysmal turnout, a sense of remoteness from government, and the marginalisation of the young, the poor, the non-tertiary-educated, people without a settled home and racial minorities. The politics were obvious: these were just the sort of people who depended most on the state supports that neoliberals were trying to dismantle.

The dissenting Labor members also pointed out that a survey of Coalition candidates for the 1996 election found that just under half (44 per cent) supported compulsory voting.[5] Many of these would have been Nationals, both because it was National Party policy and from conviction. The Liberal member for Kooyong, Petro Georgiou, who was not a member of the JSCEM, fought hard against the proposal inside the party. In 1996, as a new MP, he had put the case for compulsory voting: 'to overturn [it] would give the community an unequivocal signal that we as society's elected representatives have diminished our commitment to voting as a civic duty.'[6]

John Howard did not take up the committee's recommendation. Nevertheless, his government did break with Australia's tradition of compulsory voting for the election of delegates to the 1998 Constitutional Convention. In April 1993 Paul Keating had appointed a Republic Advisory Committee as the first step towards Australia becoming a republic. The last step would be a referendum, but by then Keating had lost the 1996 election to Howard. Keating had proposed an indicative plebiscite or non-binding vote on the question of whether Australia should become a republic. Howard instead proposed a Constitutional

Convention to determine a referendum question, with half the delegates elected and half appointed by the government.

As parliamentary secretary to the prime minister, Nick Minchin was given the task of organising the convention, and he persuaded the government that the delegates should be elected by a voluntary postal vote. The government's main argument was that it would be cheaper. Labor fought back, suspecting that the government was using this vote to test the waters for voluntary voting at federal elections.

John Faulkner told the Senate that submissions to the Senate Standing Committee on Legal and Constitutional Affairs overwhelmingly supported a compulsory vote for the delegates.

> Compulsory voting is the hallmark of our democratic electoral system. It is what empowers people in the Australian democratic process. Everyone has a stake in the outcome and we believe that it is essential in our democracy...we in the Labor Party will never back away from the Australian ballot—a compulsory attendance, secret ballot which is the Australian way of voting.[7]

In the House the Labor member for Banks, Daryl Melham, echoed early conservative arguments for compulsory voting. The system, he said, gave power to the centre to determine political outcomes.

> [A] voluntary ballot is flawed. It encourages political opponents to spend time drumming up support amongst their own supporters rather than amongst the general community—particularly those who are yet to make up their minds. If the Prime Minister is serious about building a consensus across the Australian people either for or against the republic, then it is these middle of the road swinging voters who must be convinced to vote one way or the other. It is this very dynamic that is at work in our compulsory parliamentary elections. It is what determines who wins and loses government.[8]

Although the Senate twice passed amendments to make the vote for delegates compulsory and at polling booths, the government would not relent, and seemed likely to let the convention lapse along with the push for a republic. To prevent the momentum to a republic stalling, the Greens decided to support the government and the legislation passed. When the vote for delegates was held, only 46.92 per cent of people on the electoral roll participated.[9] The convention went ahead and so did the referendum. It was compulsory to vote in the referendum and the turnout was 95.1 per cent. The referendum question, whether Australia should become a republic with a president appointed by the parliament, split republican supporters. Many who wanted the president chosen by the people voted No and the referendum was lost.

In 1997 and again in 2001 the JSCEM received submissions on voluntary voting, but didn't pursue the issue. But in 2004 it did recommend that a full and separate inquiry be held into voluntary and compulsory voting.[10] The Coalition had just won control of the Senate and there was media speculation that the voluntary-voting zealots would try again. Minchin was cautious: it had not been one of the policies the government took to the election, and the party was divided on it. Howard said that, although he personally supported voluntary voting, he believed that most Australians, including many Liberals, did not want fundamental change to our voting system.[11]

But Minchin hadn't given up—hence the JSCEM recommendation of an inquiry. It would, he said, 'be the task of those of us who want to rid our voting system of the blight of compulsion, to persuade the Coalition to take such a policy to the '07 election, for implementation if we are once again re-elected'. Control of the Senate, however, tempted Howard to destruction as he pursued his own longstanding passion: a major overhaul of industrial relations. His WorkChoices laws passed the Senate, and he lost the 2007 election to Kevin Rudd and Labor in a landslide.[12] Just before he retired from the Senate in 2011, Minchin reflected ruefully on the failure of his campaign for voluntary voting. His one achievement was to make voting for the Constitutional Convention voluntary: 'But I had to fight for that.'[13]

There was another brief flurry in 2013 when Campbell Newman, the newly elected premier of Queensland, released a discussion paper on electoral reform which included getting rid of compulsory voting.[14] But his government was fighting battles on so many fronts that this was never a priority and Newman lost office at the next election.

Repealing compulsory voting is a minority position on the right of Australian politics. The National Party, Labor, the Greens and much of the Liberal Party all support compulsory voting. One Nation doesn't have a position. On this issue at least, our politicians reflect Australian public opinion. Since 1967 the Australian Election Survey has generally found support for compulsory voting to be over 70 per cent. A survey in 2007 found that only 8 of the 23 per cent who opposed compulsory voting did so strongly, compared with half of the 77 per cent who supported it.[15]

The 1996 JSCEM cited an AGB McNair survey which found that 88 per cent of Australians would be 'likely' or 'very likely' to vote if voting were to be made voluntary. 'If the health of a democracy is to be judged by the level of voter turnout,' it concluded, 'in Australia there would seem to be no reason to fear voluntary voting.'[16] But this misses the point. These surveys are of voters who have been voting all their adult lives, for whom it is a baked-in habit. The big question is about new voters. Without compulsion, would so many acquire the habit?

The pushback against compulsory voting was accompanied by two other attempts by the Howard government to shrink the Australian electorate. The first was to follow the example of some American states and disenfranchise all prisoners. Under law at the time only those serving a sentence of three years or more lost their right to vote. Breaking the law, all prisoners had broken the social contract and so must forfeit their right to vote, the argument went. The Howard government also wanted to reduce the time after the writs were issued for voters to enrol or change their details to the close of the same day for new enrolments, and the close of day three for changes to details. The argument for this was that it would reduce the pressure of last-minute enrolments on the AEC, giving it the time it needed to check applicants' details and so protect the integrity of the roll. The argument against was that it would keep many voters, especially the young, off the rolls.

Both of these changes were recommended in the 1997 JSCEM report, alongside the abolition of compulsory voting. As the balance in the Liberal Party's broad church shifted from liberal to conservative, the party seemed to be taking cues from the Republicans in the United States, who have made voter suppression an artform. In 2006, with control of the Senate, the Howard government was able to legislate these changes; however, they have not survived. Both were challenged in the High Court, which found that parliament's power over the franchise was limited by the constitution's requirement that it be 'directly chosen by the people', and in 2010 Labor restored the status quo.[17]

The prisoner ban was challenged by an indigenous woman, Vicki Roach, who was serving a six-year sentence for burglary. In the United States the disenfranchisement of prisoners has greatest impact on African-Americans, who are disproportionately imprisoned. The same is true here for indigenous Australians, who represent more than a quarter of prisoners but only 2 per cent of the population.[18] The High Court upheld the power of the parliament to limit prisoners' voting rights under the earlier legislation, but not to abolish them altogether. Although our founding fathers had left the franchise to the parliament to determine, the High Court found that the constitution did indeed provide some protection of the rights of Australian voters against incursions from right-wing warriors.

In 2018 the Coalition-dominated JSCEM made another recommendation from the American Republican Party's playbook of voter suppression: that voters be required to show identification at polling booths, in order to guard against electoral fraud and multiple voting. The recommendation ignored the fact that voter ID would not prevent multiple voting (one can show ID twice); that most cases of multiple voting are caused by the confusions of age and poor English; that there is little evidence of electoral fraud; and that when the Queensland LNP government of Campbell Newman introduced such a requirement, turnout dropped. The report argued that it would mitigate 'the current mistrust of politicians and the democratic process by the voting public'.[19] But voter fraud and doubts about the integrity of the electoral process have little to do with the current mistrust. It is rather the self-interested and irresponsible behaviour of some of those whom the process elects. Look to the beams in one's own eyes, members and senators, not the mote of fraudulent voters.

16

AUSTRALIAN ELECTION DAYS

'THE SPIRIT OF Holiday hovers over our election boxes,' David Malouf declared in his 1998 Boyer Lectures, echoing the remark in 1902 of another Queenslander, Senator Thomas Glassey, that election days were looked forward to as 'a sort of holiday'. Malouf went on: 'Voting for us is a family occasion, a duty fulfilled, as often as not, on the way to the beach, so that children early get a sense of it as an obligation, but a light one, a duty casually undertaken.' As 'the guardian angel of our democracy, it seems preferable, and might even be more reliable, than the three or four bored paratroopers who descend to protect the ballot boxes in even the smallest village in a place as politically sophisticated as Italy'.[1] The combination of Saturday and compulsory voting creates the distinctive holiday spirit of Australian election days.

Here is Don Charlwood's description of the 1928 federal-election day in the Victorian seaside town of Frankston in his classic novel *All the Green Year* (1965). It is only the second since compulsory voting has been introduced. Bored and searching for distraction on a Saturday afternoon, the thirteen-year-old protagonist, Charlie, drifts to the

Mechanics Institute Hall on the edge of the bay.

> In their own slow way, polling days were interesting. All the peculiar people we didn't see for months at a time came out like insects from under lifted stones. There were those like the Misses Ferguson who never stopped chewing aspirin while they were among other people and always spoke from behind handkerchiefs soaked in eucalyptus. And there was Mrs Rolls, an extremely proud woman who hardly ever came out because she was so ashamed of her husband's drinking…
>
> At the Mechanics' door Mr Turnbull was handing out How to Vote cards for the party which I knew stood for authority and respectability and such other proper things. Stinger Wray's father was handing out cards for the working man and 'social justice'.
>
> Mr Turnbull wore a heavy overcoat and a bowler hat…and looked down importantly from a great height. Mr Wray was hatless and wore a reversible rubber raincoat. His boots were dirty and from his face you could tell that he believed life had done him great wrongs.
>
> It might have made the day a bit more interesting if they had argued, but I was disappointed to see that they seemed on quite friendly terms. Most people took a card from each of them, as if they were going to vote for both sides. It was all peaceful and dull.

Distraction appears with Mr Mathias, an eccentric old man who lives in the bush and is suspected of being a Bolshevik. He takes the two How to Vote cards and tears both to pieces, shouting, 'Do you know what I think of compulsory voting?' But he goes into the booth nevertheless.[2]

Just look at how much young Charlie learns from hanging about the polling booth: that all adults, even the reclusive, must vote; that

Australian politics is primarily organised around class, as it was for much of the twentieth century; that many people don't let on how they vote; that no matter what their political differences, people remain civil to each other, even friendly; and that the height of political disruption is a cranky old man tearing up his how-to-vote cards.

When I was teaching first-year Australian politics I would ask students in the first tutorial for their earliest political memory. It was a great warm-up exercise, as there was no right or wrong answer and we all learned a bit about each other. The most common memory was going with parents to vote, many to their school, where familiar classrooms had been repurposed for the occasion. Here, where children learn the rudiments of their future adult civic responsibilities, they see them enacted in a familiar community setting.[3] It was the beginning of their political learning as they asked their parents what voting was, why they had to do it, who they were voting for. Along with lessons about citizenship they also began to develop political attitudes; to learn the traditions of their family's party loyalties, and where these stood in the general scheme of things; and to have an investment in the outcome.

Today's polling booths are more colourful than the rather drab Frankston Mechanics Institute of 1928. Nowadays they are decked with corflutes, balloons and banners, and rival teams hand out how-to-vote cards while wearing bright T-shirts: red, blue, green, orange, purple, white. Young buskers may be entertaining the queues, and many polling booths will be selling food and drink. Some of the how-to-vote cards are now also in languages other than English; and there are younger voters. In 1973 the Whitlam government dropped the voting age from twenty-one to eighteen, the age at which young men were being conscripted to fight in Vietnam.

The polling booths too are different, no longer made of wood. Colin Hughes, the first Commonwealth electoral commissioner, who shared

William Boothby's attention to practical detail, proudly recounted how the commission replaced the heavy materials for voting compartments with cardboard screens. Voting booths made from wood, and later polypropylene and aluminium, were heavy and difficult to store, repair and transport. They created a barrier to the employment of women, and an incentive to industrial pressure from the storemen and carriers' union at election times. Cardboard screens saved on transport, storage and cleaning, secured freedom from industrial muscle, and enhanced equal-employment opportunities. 'The one problem was environmentalists…There was great public concern about the fate of so much forest product after polling day.' So they instituted recycling programmes.[4]

Colin Hughes's careful recounting of the detail of this decision reminds us just what a giant logistical exercise it is to organise an Australian election day, the greatest required during peacetime. For the 2016 federal election there were more than seven thousand polling places, furnished with 120,000 voting screens, a hundred thousand pencils, 140 kilometres of string (to stop pencil pilfering), sixty thousand ballot boxes and thirteen thousand recycling bins. There were also six hundred early voting centres, and forty-one mobile teams which visited four hundred remote locations by land, sea and air. The cultural and linguistic diversity of the electorate was accommodated by explanatory material being available in twenty-seven non-indigenous and thirteen indigenous languages, as well as in large-print, braille and audio versions. And all this was administered by more than seventy-five thousand polling clerks. The AEC must deal, too, with many more parties than its predecessor in 1928: fifty-seven in 2016, whereas Mr Turnbull and Stinger Wray's dad were the only two canvassers at the Frankston polling booth.[5]

*

Most polling booths are in community centres, school and church halls, or sporting clubs. Over the years volunteers have taken advantage of the fundraising possibilities of large numbers of people passing through their doors on election days, beginning with stalls selling cakes, jams and crafts.

In the 1980s, with the advent of large portable gas barbecues, mass sausage sizzles became a common feature of community events, including elections. For many voters since, buying a barbecued sausage in a bread roll or slice of white bread with fried onions, tomato sauce or mustard outside the polling booth is part of their election-day ritual.

At the 2010 Queensland election some Brisbane friends set up a website for groups to register their election-day fundraising offerings. Calling itself Snagvotes, the group's underlying objective was 'to celebrate our democracy, encourage participation in the democratic process and offer support for community groups and volunteers that run sausage sizzles and stalls on election day. The message is "Get together with your community and enjoy a sausage on election day—a great Australian tradition."' The website took off. Facebook and Twitter accounts followed, as did other websites and Google-linked maps to show the offerings at the different booths and guide voters' decisions about where to vote. A year or so later these fundraising sausages began to be called 'democracy sausages', and in 2016 the phrase was selected as word of the year by the Australian National Dictionary Centre.[6]

Since the sizzled sausage has replaced the meat pie as the typical Australian street food, being able and willing to eat one in public has become a job requirement for politicians. It demonstrates their egalitarian credentials, and ridicule awaits those who fail, as Bill Shorten did on the 2016 election day. At Strathfield North Public School, Shorten screwed up his eyes and bit into the side of his sausage in a roll. Didn't he know he should have started at one end? Clearly, social media concluded, he had never grabbed his weekend breakfast at Bunnings.[7]

It is even more dangerous to refuse one, as Malcolm Turnbull learned a year later. He was visiting Lismore to inspect flood damage when a kind volunteer from the Country Women's Association offered him a sausage on bread on a paper plate. 'That's lovely, that's very kind of you,' he said, 'but I think I am running around a bit much to be eating that,' and he awkwardly put it back on the table.[8] He too had shown himself to be no ordinary bloke.

The democracy sausage has bestowed on polling booths a little of the carnival atmosphere of the early election days and released a playful spirit. In 2016 cake stalls sold Malcolm Turnovers, Bill Shortbreads and Jacqui Lambingtons.[9] With rich visual and punning possibilities, it has helped to engage the social-media generation.

At the 2016 election five of Australia's embassies and consulates put on sausage sizzles for homesick voters.[10] After 1952 many Australian embassies and consulates were able to issue postal votes directly to Australian electors who were overseas. Instead of the ballot papers being sent and returned through the post, the papers were provided in person, witnessed, filled in and returned, all on the spot. This is how I cast my first vote, in December 1972, making the trip to London's Australia House from Oxford, where I was studying. Four years later on-the-spot postal voting was available at forty-two of Australia's overseas missions.[11]

At the 2004 election around sixty-four thousand Australians voted from overseas.[12] From 1996 until 2013 Australia House in London recorded the most votes of any single polling booth, as expats, backpackers and other assorted travellers made their way to the triangular Beaux-Arts building between Aldwych and the Strand.[13] But there was no sausage sizzle, complained a disgruntled voter after one visit.[14]

*

I went to my first election-night party in 1975. It was a gloomy affair somewhere in Gippsland as we learned that Whitlam had been thrashed. During the 1980s and 1990s my family would watch the federal-election results and the AFL grand final with the same families and with much the same range of emotions, from triumphant glee to sombre resignation. The adults would cheer and jeer and drink, while the kids would rattle around. Since it was Saturday night, they were allowed to stay up late.

In earlier days, before television and wireless, election crowds would gather outside newspaper buildings and post offices, where results were posted as they were telegraphed in. Later, people at home might listen to the wireless. John Howard has vivid memories of how his family spent the 1949 election night, which brought his hero Robert Menzies to power. They went to the pictures, as they did most Saturday nights. During the screening of the second feature a slide on the screen announced, 'L-CP takes early poll lead.' The win was confirmed on the wireless when they got home.[15] Party workers got together at local halls, but election nights were not widely seen as opportunities for private socialising with friends, no matter whether one expected to win or lose.

This began to change with the arrival of television in 1956. The first election after its debut was in November 1958. The state-based television channels were not very skilled at live-to-air telecasting, and by today's standards the presentation was clunky. In Sydney and Melbourne the ABC presented live coverage from both states' tally rooms, with interstate results phoned in. Primitive graphics displayed the fortunes of the parties, and panels of pundits and politicians discussed the results. The commercial channels also provided varying degrees of live coverage.[16]

Television sets were far from ubiquitous in 1958, and many watched the results come in at the house of a friend with a set. Thus was born the private election-night party, friends gathering early on Saturday night to eat and drink and wait for the numbers. By the end of the 1960s, these were common enough for David Williamson to write a play about one, *Don's Party*.

It is the night of the 1969 election. Labor is on the ascendant under its new leader, Gough Whitlam, and schoolteacher Don Henderson and his wife, Cath, are hosting a party at their house in Sydney's northern suburbs, hoping to celebrate Labor's first victory since Chifley lost to Menzies in 1949. As it becomes clear that, despite a swing, Labor will lose yet again, the tempo of the drinking increases, tempers rise and the men start behaving very badly indeed towards the women.

The television in the Henderson house is tuned to the National Tally Room in Canberra. Until the early 1960s, each state had its own official tally room, reporting the state results. The major newspaper chains, however, had established national tally rooms, which pushed the government's electoral branch to set up its own in Canberra. For the 1963 election the tally room was in Albert Hall on Commonwealth Avenue for the first time. Its stage was modified to accommodate the two-storey-high wooden tally board. It broadcast to Canberra, Sydney and Melbourne.[17]

For the next fifty years the National Tally Room in Canberra was the focal point of election-night communication, growing to accommodate over three hundred press, radio and television journalists, and with four purpose-built studios where panels of pundits and politicians would dissect the unfolding results and make their predictions. In the 1960s and 1970s political-science academics such as Sydney University's Henry Mayer and the ANU's Don Aitkin were frequent contributors, though these days academics are rarely seen on the panels, which are composed mainly of politicians and political journalists. Computer-driven systems gradually replaced the manually operated tally board and the telephone lines.

In 2007, when the federal Joint Standing Committee on Electoral Matters reviewed the future of the National Tally Room, it found strong attachment among voters to the drama and excitement it generated. Many said it symbolised the transparency of the electoral process. A Virtual Tally Room had been in operation since 1998; and in 2013, after the major media outlets declared they would no longer attend the National Tally Room on election night, the AEC decided to close it. Saturday-night television coverage of elections has increasingly sophisticated graphics, live crosses to jubilant and subdued candidates in pubs and clubrooms across the country, and on the ABC the animated yet even-handed commentary of Antony Green.[18]

In recent years the civic rituals of Saturday voting have been somewhat undermined by the greatly increased availability—and popularity—of pre-poll voting. Three different forms of early voting are available to Australian voters: postal votes; votes at mobile booths, where electoral officials visit hospitals, homes for the elderly, prisons and some remote locations in the days leading up to an election; and early votes at designated polling booths, including at overseas embassies. Before 2010 people wanting to vote early had to sign a declaration that they were unable to vote on election day, and these votes, along with postal and other mobile votes, were counted separately. Now pre-pollers are simply asked if they are unable to vote on polling day.

In 2009 the JSCEM recommended that pre-poll votes no longer be treated as declaration votes, but as ordinary votes, which meant that they can be counted on election night. The reasons were a mixture of administrative efficiency and democratic commitment. Saturdays were no longer the quiet half-day holidays of the early twentieth century. Many more people worked, shops were open in the afternoon, and more people were travelling.[19] These changes were in place for the

2010 election, but only 8 per cent of voters took advantage of them. Gradually the word has spread, aided by the state election authorities following suit and more early polling places being available. At the 2013 federal election, 16.9 per cent cast a pre-poll vote; predictions are that the figure may soon be more than 50 per cent.[20]

Pre-polling makes life difficult for the political parties, who now have to hand out how-to-vote cards for weeks before polling day; and it alters the dynamics of the campaign, considerably dampening the impact of a dramatic revelation on poll eve. But its greatest change may be to our Saturday festivals of democracy, when we line up with the motley crew of our fellow citizens to vote.

Perhaps the democracy sausage will save the day. Here is one blogger on her decision to forgo pre-polling at the 2013 federal election:

> I was going to complete my vote at an early polling booth near work during the week until I stumbled upon the website which mapped out the election sausage sizzle locations and found that the primary school near where I am house sitting was one…As I walked down I felt such a sense of community. Here I was walking along ahead and behind other groups doing the same—families, housemates, singles—about to participate in our democratic right and have a say in the leadership of our great and lucky country.[21]

17

OF PLEBISCITES AND SURVEYS

AT THE END of 2017 a voluntary postal survey was held on the question of same-sex marriage. Australians on the electoral roll were invited to answer Yes or No to the simple question: 'Should the law be changed to allow same-sex couples to marry?' The government promised that if more people answered Yes than No, it would change the law.

This very peculiar and roundabout process was not a referendum, as marriage was not defined by the constitution. Nor was it a plebiscite, and the government was not legally bound to act on the outcome. Rather, it was a survey of opinion. Participation was not compulsory, and instead of being administered by the AEC the survey was administered by the Australian Bureau of Statistics (ABS). It was all very ad hoc, as the Coalition government strove to manage its deep internal differences over the meaning of marriage.

Opponents of same-sex marriage hoped for a low-key campaign and a low turnout. They were wrong: 79.5 per cent of enrolled electors returned their surveys and of these 61.6 per cent voted Yes.[1] As well, the Yes campaign had through its enrolment campaigns added nearly one hundred thousand new voters to the electoral roll.

The legalisation of marriage between same-sex couples had been on the federal political agenda for more than a decade. In 2004 John Howard's government had amended the Marriage Act to define marriage as the union between a man and a woman. Between then and 2017 there were twenty-two unsuccessful attempts to introduce legislation to legalise same-sex marriage.[2] During this time public opinion shifted in favour and by 2016 opinion polls were regularly finding levels of support of 60 per cent and more.[3]

Opinions in the general public, however, had shifted faster than opinions in the parliament, and especially in the governing Coalition, where a solid group of religious believers remained staunchly opposed. Under Tony Abbott's prime ministership there was no chance of progress, but after Malcolm Turnbull successfully challenged him for the top job, progress was expected. Turnbull's support for same-sex marriage was well-known, and in his campaign for re-election in 2016 he promised a plebiscite on the question.

Plebiscites should not be confused with the referenda required to amend our constitution. A proposed constitutional amendment must first pass both houses of parliament with an absolute majority. It is then put to a compulsory vote of the people, who are asked simply Yes or No. To succeed, an absolute majority is required in a majority of the states, and the result binds the parliament. There is no other way to amend the constitution. Plebiscites, by contrast, are non-binding and legislation is still required to change the law.

Malcolm Turnbull's strategy of dealing with an internal party conflict by outsourcing the decision to the voters did have a precedent: Billy Hughes's plebiscites on conscription during World War One (although these are frequently referred to as referenda). When he was unable to overcome the strong opposition in the Labor Party to conscription for overseas service, Hughes appealed over the party to the people. The appeal failed and the Labor Party split. It was a disastrous outcome, and it left a legacy of bitterness and sectarian division.

We have had one other plebiscite in our history, on the question of what should replace 'God Save the Queen' as Australia's national anthem. In 1974 Gough Whitlam asked the ABS to conduct a national opinion poll on the question, and in 1977 Liberal Prime Minister Malcolm Fraser conducted a plebiscite on the same question, with a preferential choice of four: 'God Save the Queen', 'Waltzing Matilda', 'Advance Australia Fair' and 'Song of Australia'. As it was held in conjunction with four referenda questions, the response was high, with over seven million of the 8.4 million people on the roll choosing to vote, and 'Advance Australia Fair' the clear winner.[4]

After Turnbull's Coalition government scraped back in at the 2016 election, it introduced legislation for the promised plebiscite, which was rejected by the Senate. Supporters of same-sex marriage argued that parliament had the power to amend the Marriage Act and should just get on with it, and that a plebiscite would involve a distressing and harmful campaign. Supporters of traditional marriage within the Coalition were hoping the government, having attempted to fulfil its promise, would let the legislation lapse. But the issue itself would not go away.

Four private member's bills had been introduced since the election, and they would keep being bowled up.[5] Labor was promising to introduce legislation if it won government, so it would certainly be an issue at the next election. As well, some Coalition members were vocal supporters of the change, including the member for the Far North Queensland electorate of Leichhardt, Warren Entsch, who introduced a private member's bill in 2015, and the former Human Rights Commissioner and proudly gay man Tim Wilson. The issue had become a major distraction for the government and needed to be dealt with before the next election. Peter Dutton, himself a strong supporter of traditional marriage, came up with the ingenious solution of a voluntary postal survey conducted by the ABS.

The big advantage of this was that it bypassed parliament. Legislation was required for a plebiscite conducted by the AEC, but not for the government to direct the ABS to collect 'statistical information about the proportion of electors who wish to express a view about whether the law should be changed to allow same-sex couples to marry'. To fund the survey, the government used an ad hoc arrangement which allows the finance minister to make up to $295 million available in certain circumstances.[6] This and the role of the ABS were both subject to High Court challenges, but they survived.

Technically the ABS was conducting a postal survey, but it was talked of as if it were a vote. The ABS website invited participants to 'have your say'.[7] Giving an opinion in a survey and casting a vote are very different actions. A vote has agency, power, efficacy. It conveys authority from us, the electors, to our parliamentary representatives who, in their turn, transfer authority to the government. Our votes constitute our democracy. A survey has no intrinsic connection to democracy at all. It simply collects information about us: we hold these views; we earn this much money; we have this blood type. Our opinions are attributes, not actions.

The government promised that it would heed the resulting collective opinion, but it was not constitutionally bound to do so. Parliament still had to vote on it, as it had had the power to do all along. Prominent supporters of traditional marriage like Tony Abbott and Eric Abetz made clear that they would not feel bound by the results.

Because the survey was postal, there was no guarantee of secrecy. Forms were received by post and filled in anywhere. There was even provision for 'a trusted person' to complete the survey for you. The instructions on the ABS website describe this as 'a private arrangement between you and a person whom you trust', adding that 'A person cannot self-nominate.'[8] But as there was no formal process of nomination, how would the ABS know?

Compounding problems with secrecy, survey forms were entrusted to the insecure medium of the post. Each survey return was barcoded to link it to a particular elector, so that an elector could request another form should theirs not turn up. If the form was stolen from their post box, or kitchen table, filled in and returned by someone else, then that unlucky respondent simply missed out on their 'vote'. Improvising in the face of unforeseen risks, the ABS advised people not to post images of their survey forms on social media before sending them back lest someone reproduce its barcode and steal their vote.[9]

This seemed the least likely of the many possible intercepts between a respondent and their form. The banks of letterboxes outside blocks of flats and apartments provided easy pickings for zealots and mischief-makers. Bundles of dumped forms destined for left-leaning suburbs were found in laneways, and some people in share houses filled out forms for long-departed tenants.[10]

Adding to the irregularity and uncertainty of the process were the eight weeks between the ABS beginning to send out the forms and the final date for their return. Eight weeks! If this really was a survey, an experienced polling agency could have done it in a week, more cheaply, and with far less sound and fury. But then the people would not all have had the chance to 'have their say'. The divisive and hurtful debate was stretched out, as both sides upped the emotional rhetoric to persuade those who hadn't returned their surveys to do so.

Some same-sex marriage supporters advocated a boycott. The former High Court judge Michael Kirby said he would take no part in the process. Other minority groups had not had their rights referred to the people. Plebiscites were not held on the legal rights of Aboriginal people, on the advancement of women's legal rights, nor on the demolition of White Australia, he said, and he wanted no part of this irregular and 'unacceptable improvisation'.[11] When it was clear that the survey was going to happen, however, most changed their position and urged people to participate.

Ignoring the opinion polls, some opponents hoped that the silent majority supported traditional marriage, or at least that the older, more conservative, better organised people of this silent majority would be more likely to post back their forms than the young, who mostly supported same-sex marriage but rarely used snail mail.[12] But the No side was not only wrong; it was spectacularly out-campaigned. Celebrities such as Magda Szubanski, Ian Thorpe, Jimmy Barnes, Cate Blanchett and Bindi Irwin used social media to support the cause, and openly gay business leaders like Alan Joyce of Qantas and Jennifer Westacott of the Business Council of Australia gave vocal support.[13] Labor and Green politicians were out in force, whereas many Liberal supporters of traditional marriage barely campaigned at all.

The Yes side also had a highly recognisable visual symbol. Pride rainbows were everywhere: flags, painted faces, headbands, streamers, balloons, cupcakes, posters, decorated houses. A child could draw one with seven crayons, and many did. The rainbows gave a festive, party feel to what was an otherwise highly charged, emotional and distressing process for LGBTQI people and their friends and families.

The Yes campaign began well before the surveys were posted, urging people to register and to update their details. The young, who supported same-sex marriage most strongly, were least likely to be on the electoral roll. They were also most likely, even if registered, to have recently changed address and so to not receive their form. The first task was to make sure they were on the roll. As well as the usual urging from the AEC and political organisations, entertainment venues hosted 'rego parties' with enrolment forms, envelopes and iPads to make the process easy. At one popular Newcastle nightclub staff took their iPads down the queue of waiting punters so they could check that their enrolment details were up to date.[14]

The campaign was hugely successful. Between 8 August 2017, when it became clear that the survey would happen, and 24 August, when changes to the roll closed, the AEC processed a total of 933,592 enrolment transactions, a third more than before the 2016 election, including ninety-eight thousand new enrolments, sixty-five thousand of them eighteen- to twenty-four-year-olds. It was, said the AEC, 'extraordinary'.

Yes campaigners were elated, but for the conservatives in the Coalition it looked like an own goal. All these young, progressive voters were now on the roll for the next election. It was, said one disgruntled Liberal MP, something those who pushed for the plebiscite should have been able to foresee: 'Young people care more about same-sex marriage than they do about elections. They're more interested in whether their friends can get married than choosing between Malcolm Turnbull and Bill Shorten.'[15]

Another deviation from our electoral practices in this improvised process was the mode of announcement. No groups gathered round the television to watch the results come in a few hours after the poll closed. Instead, the result was announced by the ABS Chief Statistician, David Kalisch, at a 10 a.m. press conference eight days after the cut-off date for the receipt of surveys. As 'It is probably the only time millions of Australians will gather to hear from the Australian statistician,' he took the opportunity to tell them a little about the role of the ABS, making the country wait five minutes for the result.

Yes had won. Kalisch said that the turnout of 79.5 per cent was 'outstanding for a voluntary survey and well above other voluntary exercises conducted around the world', and he noted that the participation rate of eighteen- and nineteen-year-olds was 78 per cent.[16] 'Love has had a landslide victory,' said the co-chair of the Equality Campaign, Alex Greenwich, speaking from one of the many rainbow-festooned public parties held in anticipation of victory.[17]

Three weeks later same-sex marriage was legal. The bill, introduced by a Liberal senator from Western Australia, Dean Smith, achieved massive cross-party support, though some MPs and senators voted No, and others abstained, including Tony Abbott, whose electorate of Warringah had voted 75 per cent Yes. When the division was called, he headed for the door. Scott Morrison, Barnaby Joyce and around a dozen others in the House of Representatives also abstained. Reportedly, it was a way they could accommodate both their personal views on same-sex marriage and the clear majority Yes vote in the postal survey.[18]

Peter Dutton, the chief architect of the postal survey and vocal supporter of traditional marriage, was gracious in defeat:

> given the voluntary expression of view by 8 million people, and the emphatic 'yes' vote that followed in the Parliament, the legitimacy given to this significant social change was infinitely greater than a shabby vote in the Parliament with people crossing the floor. The 5 million who hold a legitimate 'no' view would have felt cheated and would not have accepted the process and outcome.

Dutton was adamant, though, that the postal-vote process should not be used again. It was, he said, the nature of the issue—a change to one of society's foundation stones—that dictated this 'break glass option'.[19] (The mixed metaphor is his.) We'll see.

Despite its many deviations from Australia's electoral traditions, this voluntary, non-secret ballot ended up confirming them. Our years of compulsory voting had impressed on people the importance of their participation; activists ran a successful enrolment drive that registered a huge number of new voters; and our majoritarian traditions meant that the losers accepted the result. It also showed the limits in Australia of religious mobilisation around moral issues. The silent majority in their traditional suburban marriages, who did not feel threatened or offended by the idea of same-sex marriage, backed tolerance.

18

WE ARE GOOD AT ELECTIONS

IN THE MIDDLE of the nineteenth century the south-eastern mainland states of Australia gave every man a vote, and the secret Australian ballot transformed voting practices. In the 1890s, South and Western Australia followed New Zealand in giving women the vote. These democratic achievements led the world and shaped the nation created in 1901 when the colonies federated. Democracy was in its blood and the experiments continued.

Australia was the first nation to give women the right to stand for parliament, and the first to establish a national non-partisan electoral machinery. It paid close attention to potential barriers to voting of distance, literacy and mobility. It made it compulsory to be on the electoral roll, legislated for Saturday polling days and introduced preferential voting. In his 1921 comparative study of modern democracies the British liberal political historian James Bryce wrote that this 'newest of all the democracies...has travelled farthest and fastest along the road which leads to the unlimited rule of the multitude'.[1]

All this was achieved well before 1924, when Australia adopted compulsory voting. Advocacy for compulsory voting began in the last few decades of the nineteenth century but the reform faced a number of hurdles: its sheer novelty, its break with British precedent, practical considerations about enforcement, and Labor's stubborn opposition to postal voting. A few people worried about the infringement of liberty but not many, and none mounted a well-developed philosophical case against the government compelling people to vote.

Federalism complicated matters, as did World War One, but the deep currents of Australian political life were carrying us forward to the day in July 1924 when we adopted compulsory voting. This was not, as has sometimes been claimed, an accidental decision carelessly made by inattentive parliamentarians, but the result of Australia's confidence in government, its commitment to majoritarian democracy and its willingness to experiment with electoral matters.

Our early federal politicians were proud of Australia's reputation as a democratic laboratory. Determined to create a fair and accessible electoral system, they tinkered away until they got it right. Between 1901 and 1924 parliament passed twenty-four acts on electoral matters, as well as considering another twelve unsuccessful bills.[2] Subsequently, the spirit of incremental innovation was applied to the Senate, with the introduction of proportional representation in 1948, and more recently in the tinkering with above- and below-the-line voting. As problems emerge and priorities change, Australian politicians have been willing to innovate.

Colonial governments ran elections in Australia as they ran so much else, opening up land for settlement, building infrastructure, providing law and order, educating children. Australians might complain about venal and self-serving politicians but on the whole our history has seen us trust the government. In the middle of the nineteenth century, when manhood suffrage exponentially expanded the electorate, there was really no alternative but to employ salaried public servants to run elections and to manage the rolls. Political parties barely existed and local government was too underdeveloped to take on the tasks.

Clever, dedicated senior bureaucrats drove the rationalisation of electoral processes to make them more efficient and comprehensive. South Australia's William Boothby pioneered the running of elections by salaried public servants and introduced continuous government-initiated enrolment.[3] The Commonwealth's second Chief Electoral Officer, Ryton Campbell Oldham, persuaded Labor to introduce compulsory registration and argued that it should be accompanied by compulsory voting. Once we had adopted compulsory registration, compulsory voting was all but inevitable.

Australia's efficient non-partisan electoral administration is an important democratic achievement, protecting us from the partisan gerrymandering and voter suppression that blights elections in the United States. On the whole, Australians trust their electoral system and accept the legitimacy of its outcomes. As a result, despite the high stakes and strong passions of electoral contests, there are very few legal challenges to results.[4]

The most common argument for compulsory voting was the majoritarian one: that the elected government should represent not just the majority of those who vote but the majority of those eligible to vote. This would increase the government's legitimacy and make sure it paid attention to the interests of all the people. Similar arguments were put in support of preferential voting, which was introduced at the federal level in 1918. It prevents the election of candidates who win only a minority of the first-preference vote.

Majoritarian arguments for compulsory voting in Australia are a close companion of egalitarianism. If government is to deliver the greatest happiness to the greatest number, then the greatest number need to vote. Everyone counts as one and property has no special claims. We know from voluntary systems that the poor and marginalised are the least likely to vote, but with compulsory voting no political party can afford to ignore a substantial group of voters. Policies pitched only at the comfortable won't fly. Without compulsory voting, for example, the Liberal Party would likely have abolished Medicare long ago, relying on the fact that those who needed it most were least likely to vote.

Compulsory registration and voting also foster political engagement. Because young people reaching voting age and new citizens are compelled to vote, most pay at least minimal attention to parties, leaders and issues. There will always be some who donkey-vote or spoil their ballots, as they are free to do, but after a few elections many more will be better informed and more interested than had voting been a matter of choice rather than an obligation. Some partisan feelings are likely to have developed and voting to have become a habit.

Progressives focus on the egalitarian benefits of compulsory voting, but there are also more conservative arguments. Compulsory voting brings to the polls not just the poor and marginalised, the young and new immigrants, but busy people with better things to do with their time and no political axe to grind. It ensures that moderate citizens balance the zealots of both right and left, and creates a sensible centre concerned with matters of general public interest.

A common argument against compulsory registration and voting is that it lets political parties off the hook. Politicians as different as Billy Hughes and Nick Minchin have seen grassroots political organisation as the main means of getting out the vote: building branches, recruiting members, public meetings, personal canvassing. But, as John Mackey saw at the beginning of last century in Victoria, moral outrage is also a great motivator, especially when backed by religious conviction. In the United States gun laws, abortion, same-sex marriage, immigration and climate change are all potent mobilising issues but they are also polarising, eroding social cohesion and making the country harder to govern as noisy groups on both sides raise the emotional stakes.

Australian commentators frequently suggest that we are heading down the same path, that Australia too is subject to polarising populist forces from both left and right, and is becoming impossible to govern. Most weekends you can find such sentiments in the opinion pages of News Corp papers. I don't agree. Not only does religious belief have less political influence here than in the United States, but compulsory voting tempers the impact of the passionate and committed voters of the base with the votes of the moderate and indifferent. It lowers the emotional temperature of our politics and keeps open the sensible centre. The angry and aggrieved will always be drawn to politics, but compulsory voting ensures that they are not the main occupants of the public square. Australian elections are won and lost in the centre, and compulsory voting is the reason.

On 20 October 2018 Kerryn Phelps narrowly defeated Dave Sharma in the Wentworth by-election. The Liberals had held the seat since Menzies founded the party in 1945 and went into the contest with a margin of almost 18 per cent. The circumstances were unusual, with the by-election caused by the resignation of the sitting member, Malcolm Turnbull, after the Liberal party room turned against him and he resigned as prime minister. Nevertheless, Phelps's victory shows us another general benefit of compulsory voting: it makes it easier for new entrants, both parties and independents, to contest seats. In a short campaign, run without the backing of a major party, Phelps had to raise money, and to recruit and organise campaign workers; but she did not have to register voters or get them to the polls, just persuade them to give their vote to her.

Phelps's election victory was the result both of the shambles and division in the federal Liberal Party and of longer-term trends. One of the things political parties do in a democracy is connect ordinary people with the political elites and the processes of government, giving them a team to identify with and people who seem a bit like them at the heart of things. For some time, however, our three dominant parties, Labor, Liberal and the Country Party turned National, have been doing this for fewer and fewer people, with each suffering declines in brand loyalty.

Since 2010, the number of rusted-on, lifelong party voters has plunged. Fewer people report very strong levels of partisanship, more are splitting their vote between the House of Representatives and the Senate, and fewer are following the parties' how-to-vote cards.[5] Accompanying this loosening of party loyalties has been a general decline in trust for our major institutions in politics, business and the media.[6] Without compulsory voting, many disillusioned voters would turn away from politics altogether and stop voting; but because they have to find someone to vote for, new contestants, many from outside the established political class, enter the fray to pick up their protest and offer an alternative. This is a very good thing.

Over the past three decades or so the Greens, Pauline Hanson's One Nation Party, Bob Katter's Australian Party and Clive Palmer's short-lived Palmer United Party, as well as prominent independents like Tony Windsor, Andrew Wilkie, Cathy McGowan and Kerryn Phelps, have benefited from voters' disaffection with the parties which dominated Australian politics in the twentieth century. We might not like all of these new contestants, or agree with their positions, but compulsory voting keeps the disillusioned voters in the tent engaged in the peaceful protest of changing their vote.

It also encourages the major parties to modify their policies to try to win back some of their erstwhile supporters, as Labor is doing with the

Greens and John Howard did when One Nation began to take votes from the Coalition. Many feel that Howard shifted too far towards One Nation's policies, especially with his government's harsh treatment of asylum seekers. Howard wrote recently that he 'deliberately rejected the approach of branding her and her supporters as extreme and racist… Some of her supporters did have racist attitudes, but in my opinion the great bulk of her voters felt that they had been left behind and were "outsiders" in a generally prosperous nation.'[7]

Dealing with newcomers is painful for established politicians as they see comfortable margins eroded and career plans threatened. Unsurprisingly, there is plenty of ranting against irresponsible and divisive minorities, and hand-wringing over the difficulties of governing a fragmented nation.[8] But there are real risks to the established parties in ignoring significant groups of disillusioned supporters. Compulsory voting keeps our political system flexible, forcing political players to adapt to the shifting sentiments and interests of the majority or lose office. It ensures that no significant minority group ends up outside the political system altogether.

Australia's democratic achievements are not flawless. The disenfranchising of indigenous Australians by the first Commonwealth Franchise Act was shameful and continued for far too long into the twentieth century. Federation pushed indigenous Australians out of the new nation for more than sixty years, relegating them to the margins of the white Australian political community. Non-white overseas-born residents were also disenfranchised, but at least their children born here could vote. And voting rights in local-government elections in all states except Queensland still include various forms of property qualifications and plural voting.[9]

In one way we have gone backwards. The 1902 Franchise Bill that

Richard O'Connor introduced gave the right to vote on 'one ground only…residence in the Commonwealth of six months or over by any person of adult age'. This liberal intention was compromised by racial exclusions, but it is more generous in terms of residence than our current law, which bases the right to vote on citizenship. Permanent residents who do not become citizens cannot vote, even if they have lived here and paid taxes for years, so around a million people subject to our laws have no say in them. New Zealand, by contrast, gives the right to vote to permanent residents after a year of continuous residence.[10]

There are other democratic deficits: for example, the light regulation and poor transparency of political donations and campaign finance; or the parties' processes of preselection which determine the choice of candidates. I haven't explored these issues. My focus has been the voters, not the parties—the men and women numbering their ballot papers, rather than those standing for election. This book tells the story of why we vote as we do, not who we vote for. It is about the mechanics of our voting: who can vote, where, when, and how our votes are counted.

Compulsory voting is at the heart of this story. Australians need more than the Anzac story to understand the success of our nation. We need stories about our political institutions and traditions, and the men and women who made them. The Anzac story is so powerful not just because of its heroic content but also because it affirms qualities Australians were already proud of before the Great War: our egalitarianism and our talent for practical improvisation.

So too does the story of compulsory voting. It was the culmination of a series of practical experiments in democracy which began in the 1850s in the greenfield sites of the Australian colonies. Free of the old world's class restrictions and traditional ways of doing things, colonial political innovators embraced democracy. The federation fathers built on their achievements, creating a majoritarian electoral system with uniform rules across the nation. We did not want people in different states having different electoral rights, and we did not want political parties and politicians manipulating our electoral system for partisan advantage. Instead, we trusted government bureaucrats to run our elections efficiently and impartially.

With preferential voting and non-partisan electoral administration, compulsory voting forms a triumvirate protecting our majoritarian faith in democracy and our commitment to peaceful constitutional processes for resolving differences. From the invention of the Australian ballot to the humble democracy sausage, we have been innovators in electoral practice.

There are many reasons to be frustrated with Australian politics in the second decade of the twenty-first century, as we suffer our sixth prime minister in eight years, but our electoral system is not one of them. What the story of compulsory voting tells us is how very good we are at elections. We should celebrate it.

ACKNOWLEDGMENTS

In writing this book I have relied heavily on the work of colleagues who have made a special study of Australia's electoral history: Peter Brent, John Hirst and Marion Sawer. I would like to thank Graeme Orr, John Uhr and Antony Green for reading the manuscript, and Michael Heyward for suggesting to me that I write a book on Australia's distinctive practice of compulsory voting.

NOTES

CHAPTER 1: OUR MAJORITARIAN DEMOCRACY

1. In Europe only small players compel voters to the ballot box: Belgium, Luxembourg, Lichtenstein, Cyprus, Greece, two regions of Austria and one Swiss canton. The only other ex-British colonies in the group are Cyprus, Egypt, Fiji and Singapore. Apart from Singapore, the only Asian country in the group is Thailand. In Central and South America, however, it is the norm, with Argentina, Brazil, Bolivia, Chile, Ecuador, Peru, Panama, Costa Rica, Peru and the Dominican Republic all making voting compulsory and enforcing it. There are some other countries, such as Venezuela and the Philippines, where voting is compulsory but not enforced. Hill, 'A Great Leveller' in M. Sawer (ed.), *Elections*, 129; McAllister, *The Australian Voter*, 20.
2. The American government does not compute official figures and estimates of turnout range from 56 to 60 per cent. Penn State University Libraries, voter turnout, guides.libraries.psu.edu/post-election-2016/voter-turnout; accessed 9 October 2018.
3. United Kingdom Electoral Commission, 'EU Referendum Results'; electoralcommission.org.uk/find-information-by-subject/elections-and-referendums/past-elections-and-referendums/eu-referendum/electorate-and-count-information; accessed 9 October 2018.
4. Institute for Democracy and Electoral Assistance, 'Voter Turnout by Election Type: Canada', idea.int/data-tools/country-view/74/40; accessed 9 October 2018.
5. Australian Electoral Commission (AEC), 'Voter Turnout: 2016 House of Representatives and Senate Elections', aec.gov.au/About_AEC/research/files/voter-turnout-2016.pdf; accessed 9 October 2018.
6. G. Sawer, *Australian Federal Politics and Law*, 237.
7. Mackerras & McAllister, 'Compulsory Voting, Party Stability and Electoral Advantage in Australia', 221; McAllister, *The Australian Voter*, 21–23.
8. Reserve Bank of Australia, pre-decimal inflation calculator, rba.gov.au/calculator/annualPreDecimal.html; accessed 1 November 2018.
9. Farrell & McAllister, *The Australian Electoral System*, 143–45.
10. Phillip Hudson, 'Barack Obama Wants Compulsory Voting', *Australian*, 20 March 2015.
11. Collins, 'Political Ideology in Australia'.
12. Dinwiddy, *Bentham*.
13. Hancock, *Australia*, 71–73.
14. Hirst, *Australia's Democracy*, 314–15.
15. Overacker, *The Australian Party System*, 15.
16. Farrell & McAllister, *The Australian Electoral System*, 52.

CHAPTER 2: THE INVENTION OF THE AUSTRALIAN BALLOT

1. Hirst, 'Making Voting Secret', ch. 1.
2. This description of Australia's first election draws on Thompson, *The First Election*; Hirst, 'Making Voting Secret', 7–9.
3. *The Fortunes of Richard Mahony*, Part 3, ch. 10.
4. R. L. Knight, 'Lowe, Robert (1811–1892)', Australian Dictionary of Biography (ADB).
5. Hirst, *The Strange Birth of Colonial Democracy*, 16–29.
6. Hirst, *The Strange Birth of Colonial Democracy*, 98–103.

7 Hirst, *Australia's Democracy*, ch. 2; AEC, 'Events in Australian Electoral History', aec.gov.au/Elections/Australian_Electoral_History/reform.htm; accessed 3 October 2018. I give a later date than the AEC for the achievement of manhood suffrage in Tasmania, based on Hughes & Graham, *A Handbook of Australian Government and Politics*, 588.
8 From the *Northern Star*, a Chartist newspaper, cited in Charlton, *The Chartists*, 34.
9 Beluch, *Replenish the Earth*, 311–12; Serle, *The Golden Age*, 382.
10 Trollope, *An Autobiography*, 302.
11 McKenna, 'The Story of the Australian Ballot' in M. Sawer (ed.), *Elections*, 49.
12 Cited in Hirst, 'Making Voting Secret', 30.
13 Hirst, 'Making Voting Secret', chs 3 & 4.
14 R. S. Neale, 'Chapman, Henry Samuel (1803–1881)'; C. H. Currey, 'Denison, Sir William Thomas (1804–1871)', ADB.
15 *Argus*, *Age*, 6 February 1855, 4, 5.
16 Atkinson & Roberts, '"Men of Colour"'.
17 Brent, 'The Rise of the Returning Officer', 138–46.
18 Hirst, 'Making Voting Secret', 33–39.
19 Scott, *A Short History of Australia*, 261.

CHAPTER 3: THREE SOUTH AUSTRALIAN INNOVATORS

1 Magery, *Unbridling the Tongues of Women*, 143–44; Spence, *An Autobiography*, 23–24.
2 William Prideaux Courtney, 'Hare, Thomas', *Dictionary of National Biography*, 1901 supplement, en.wikisource.org/wiki/Hare,_Thomas_(DNB01); accessed 14 November 2018.
3 Spence, *An Autobiography*, 23–24.
4 Spence, 'A Plea for Pure Democracy'.
5 Spence at her eightieth birthday party, cited in Magery, *Unbridling the Tongues of Women*, 142.
6 Spence, *An Autobiography*, ch. 14; Magery, *Unbridling the Tongues of Women*, ch. 7.
7 Reid & Forrest, *Australia's Commonwealth Parliament*, 90–91; Farrell & McAllister, *The Australian Electoral System*, 26–27.
8 Farrell & McAllister, *The Australian Electoral System*, 25.
9 Wentworth by-election 2018, tallyroom.aec.gov.au/HouseDivisionPage-22844-152.htm; accessed 14 November 2018.
10 Farrell & McAllister, *The Australian Electoral System*, 52.
11 Taylor, 'The Early Life of Mr Justice Boothby'.
12 *Register* (Adelaide), 14 July 1903, 6.
13 1856 Electoral Act, Austlit, classic.austlii.edu.au/au/legis/sa/num_act/ea10o19v18556180; accessed 5 September 2018.
14 Brent, 'The Rise of the Returning Officer', 113–18.
15 *West Australian*, 23 September 1899, 5.
16 This section is based on Brent, 'The Rise of the Returning Officer', chs 4 & 5.
17 Brent, 'The Rise of the Returning Officer', 187–89.
18 The State Library of South Australia has a chronology which includes a range of letters for and against women getting the vote, as well as excerpts from the parliamentary debates, sutori.com/story/women-s-suffrage-in-south-australia; accessed 16 April 2018.
19 Helen Jones, 'Lee, Mary (1821–1909)', ADB.
20 Spence, *An Autobiography*, 70.
21 *South Australian Register*, 19 December 1894, 3.
22 Spence, *Autobiography*, 77.
23 *South Australian Register*, 19 December 1894, 6; Wright, *You Daughters of Freedom*, 55–57.
24 *Adelaide Observer*, 2 May 1896, 41, 24.
25 Hirst, 'Western Australia', *Oxford Companion to Australian History*, 678–79.
26 Bannon, 'South Australia' in Irving (ed.), *The Centenary Companion to Federation*, 162–65.
27 Wright, *You Daughters of Freedom*, 65–73.

CHAPTER 4: DIRECTLY CHOSEN BY THE PEOPLE
1. Hirst, *Sentimental Nation*, 160–61.
2. Reid & Forrest, *Australia's Commonwealth Parliament*, 85–87.
3. Rydon, 'Electoral Methods' in Simms (ed.), *1901*.
4. Garran, *Prosper the Commonwealth*, 143–44.
5. Simms (ed.), *1901*, ch. 1.
6. *Commonwealth Parliamentary Debates* (*CPD*), 5 June 1901, 744; Reid & Forrest, *Australia's Commonwealth Parliament*, 95.

CHAPTER 5: WOMEN IN, ABORIGINES OUT
1. *CPD*, Senate, 9 April 1902, 11450.
2. *CPD*, House of Representatives (HoR), 24 April 1902, 11969–74.
3. *CPD*, HoR, 23 April 1902, 11935; *CPD*, 9 April 1902, 11480.
4. *CPD*, HoR, 23 April 1902, 11937.
5. *CPD*, HoR, 23 April 1902, 11953.
6. *Age*, 17 June 1902, 7.
7. *CPD*, Senate, 9 April 1902, 11453.
8. *CPD*, Senate, 9 April 1902, 11467.
9. Stretton & Finnimore, 'Black Fellow Citizens', 522–23.
10. *CPD*, HoR, 24 April 1902, 11975.
11. *CPD*, Senate, 10 April 1902, 11580–82.
12. Federation Debates, Adelaide, 1897, cited in Chesterman & Galligan, *Citizens without Rights*, 71–72.
13. *CPD*, Senate, 9 April 1902, 11561.
14. *CPD*, Senate, 10 April 1902, 11580.
15. Brian de Garis, 'Matheson, Sir Alexander Peacock (1861–1929)', *Biographical Dictionary of the Australian Senate*.
16. *CPD*, Senate, 22 May 1901, 152.
17. *CPD*, Senate, 9 April 1902, 11467.
18. *CPD*, Senate, 10 April 1902, 11580–81.
19. *CPD*, Senate, 10 April 1902, 11587.
20. *CPD*, Senate, 10 April 1902, 11585 & 11586.
21. *CPD*, Senate, 10 April 1902, 11586–67.
22. *CPD*, Senate, 10 April 1902, 11582.
23. *CPD*, HoR, 24 April 1902, 11977.
24. The debate in the House of Representatives was on 24 April 1902; Higgins's amendment, *CPD*, 11977.
25. *CPD*, HoR, 24 April 1902, 11976.
26. *CPD*, HoR, 24 April 1902, 11980; Faulkner & Macintyre, *True Believers*, 24.
27. *CPD*, HoR, 24 April 1902, 11980.
28. Alfred Deakin, Diary, 24 April 1902, MS 1540/2/22, National Library of Australia.
29. *CPD*, 29 May 1902, 13002–03.
30. Reynolds, *This Whispering in Our Hearts*.
31. *CPD*, Senate, 22 May 1901, 152.
32. Roberts, 'The Brutal Truth'.
33. Robert Garran, Memo, 30 September 1905 in Chesterman & Galligan (eds), *Citizens without Rights*, 92.
34. The above three paragraphs draw on Stretton & Finnimore, 'Black Fellow Citizens'.
35. Chesterman & Galligan, *Citizens without Rights*, 103–06.
36. Chesterman & Galligan, *Citizens without Rights*, 93–94.
37. Rowse, *Indigenous and Other Australians*, 235–36.

38 The above two paragraphs draw on Chesterman & Galligan, *Citizens without Rights*, 157–62.
39 Norberry & Williams, 'Voters and the Franchise', 15–16.

CHAPTER 6: ADMINISTERING ELECTIONS IMPARTIALLY

1 Cited in G. N. Hawker, 'Boothby, William Robinson (1829–1903)', ADB.
2 *Argus*, 12 June 1901, 6.
3 It was in the Ministry for Home Affairs, 1901–17; Home and Territories, 1927–28; Home Affairs, 1928–32; and Interior after that. Hughes, 'The Bureaucratic Model', 114.
4 Hughes, 'The Bureaucratic Model'. The claim that Australia has a characteristic talent for bureaucracy was made by Davies in *Australian Democracy*, 3.
5 The University of Western Australia's (UWA) Australian Politics and Elections Database puts the 1901 roll at 987,754.
6 M. Sawer, 'Enrolling the People' in Orr et al (eds), *Realising Democracy*, 52–65; Brent, 'The Rise of the Returning Officer', 209–11.
7 GetUp Ltd versus Electoral Commissioner (2010), vol. 268, *Australian Law Reports*, 797.
8 AEC Research, 'Direct Enrolment and Direct Update: The Australian Experience', 2012, aec.gov.au/About_AEC/research/files/direct.pdf; accessed 9 April 2018. AEC, 'Direct Enrolment and Update', aec.gov.au/Enrolling_to_vote/About_Electoral_Roll/direct.htm; accessed 9 April 2018.
9 Adelaide *Advertiser*, 18 July 1903, 7.
10 Uhr, 'Rules for Representation', 225.
11 American Civil Liberties Union, Felony Disenfranchisement Map, aclu.org/issues/voting-rights/voter-restoration/felony-disenfranchisement-laws-map; accessed 11 October 2018.
12 Cited in Robert F. Kennedy Jr, 'Was the 2004 Election Stolen?', *Rolling Stone*, 1 June 2006, accessed on Common Dreams, commondreams.org/views06/0601-34.htm, 13 September 2018.
13 Anderson, *One Person, No Vote*.
14 Jelani Cobb, 'Not Every Vote Counts', *New Yorker*, 29 October 2018.
15 Cheyenne Haslett & Roey Hadar, 'North Dakota Native Americans Fight to Protect Their Right to Vote after Court Ruling', ABC News (American Broadcasting Company), 21 October 2018.
16 '2000 Presidential Election Recount in Florida', en.wikipedia.org/wiki/2000_United_States_presidential_election_recount_in_Florida; accessed 13 September 2018. I would not normally cite a Wikipedia article, but this is exceptionally detailed, well referenced and based on primary archival research.
17 'Report of the Electoral Officers Conference', *Age*, 6 July 1901, 10.
18 *CPD*, 30 July 1902, 14723–34.
19 S. 139 (3) Commonwealth Electoral Act, 1902, legislation.gov.au/Details/C1902A00019; accessed 3 April 2018; *Government Gazette*, no. 57, 19 October 1903, 685.
20 Gov.UK, 'Ways of Voting', gov.uk/voting-in-the-uk; accessed 14 November 2018.
21 Gabriella Jozwick, 'Time Off Work to Vote Should Be a Right', *Guardian*, 4 May 2011; Hannah Crouch, 'Can I Have Time Off to Vote in the General Election 2017?', *Sun*, 8 June 2017.
22 Citizens Information—Voting, citizensinformation.ie/en/government_in_ireland/elections_and_referenda/voting/registering_to_vote.html; accessed 3 April 2018.
23 Ciara Nugent, 'Why Thousands of Irish Expats Are Flying Home to Vote in the Historic Abortion Referendum', *Time*, 24 May 2018.
24 Elections Canada Online, 'A History of the Vote in Canada', elections.ca/content.aspx?section=res&dir=his&document=index&lang=e; accessed 4 April 2018.
25 National Conference of State Legislatures, Absentee and Early Voting, ncsl.org/research/elections-and-campaigns/absentee-and-early-voting.aspx#overview; accessed 4 April 2018.

26 New Zealand Government, 'Voting in an Election', govt.nz/browse/engaging-with-government/enrol-and-vote-in-an-election/voting-in-an-election; accessed 4 April 2018.
27 Orr, *The Law of Politics*, 76–80.

CHAPTER 7: COUNTING THE VOTE

1 *CPD*, 31 January 1902, 9529–43.
2 G. C. Fendley, 'Nanson, Edward John (1850–1936)', ADB; Professor Nanson, 'Parliamentary Election Bill', *Argus*, 18 August 1900, 14.
3 The mathematical reasoning is explained by Judith Homeshaw in 'Inventing Hare-Clark', 99–102.
4 *CPD*, 27 February 1902, 10405–21.
5 *CPD*, 17 July 1902, 13790–91; 23 July 1902, 14612–24.
6 B. D. Graham, 'The Choice of Voting Methods in Federal Politics, 1902–1918', 216.
7 Brett, *The Enigmatic Mr Deakin*, 292.
8 Deakin to Watson, 28 May 1906, Watson papers, MS 451/1/6, National Library of Australia; Reid & Forrest, *Australia's Commonwealth Parliament*, 114–15.
9 *CPD*, 21 August 1906, 310–24.

CHAPTER 8: EARLY ARGUMENTS OVER COMPULSORY VOTING

1 Adelaide *Advertiser*, 23 March 1961, 2, cited in John & DeBats, 'Australia's Adoption of Compulsory Voting', 67.
2 Melbourne *Herald*, 2 August 1876, 2.
3 Melbourne *Herald*, 13 October 1876, 2.
4 John & DeBats, 'Australia's Adoption of Compulsory Voting', 10.
5 *Victorian Parliamentary Debates (VPD)*, Legislative Assembly, 14 November 1888, 1957.
6 *Leader*, 27 October 1888, 28; 3 November 1888, 24.
7 *VPD*, 14 November 1888, 1958–59.
8 *Bendigo Independent*, 23 July 1906, 2.
9 John & DeBats, 'Australia's Adoption of Compulsory Voting, 18–19.
10 *VPD*, 6 December 1906, 3539.
11 *VPD*, 6 December 1906, 3538–42.
12 *Age*, 19 July 1906, 5.
13 *Sydney Morning Herald (SMH)*, 23 May 1906, 28.
14 Age, 7 March 1907, 10.
15 *SMH*, 13 July 1905, 6.
16 *Age*, 4 December 1906, 6.
17 *Age*, 4 February 1909, 8.
18 Launceston *Examiner*, 7 June 1906, 5.
19 *CPD*, 18 July 1907, 650.
20 Report of meeting of Trades Hall Council, *Argus*, 19 September 1908, 16.
21 George Prendergast, Labor's Parliamentary Leader, *Age*, 28 January 1907, 4.

CHAPTER 9: LABOR IN POWER

1 *CPD*, 4 December 1911, 2633 & 2635.
2 Arthur Hoyle, 'O'Malley, King (1858–1953)', ADB.
3 Commonwealth Electoral Act (1911), s. 139.
4 *CPD*, 7 December 1911, 39389.
5 *CPD*, 5 December 1905, 3720; 6 December 1905, 3808.
6 *CPD*, 20 October 1911, 1684.

7   *CPD*, 6 December 1911, 3811.
8   M. Sawer, 'Enrolling the People', 57.
9   Brett, *Robert Menzies' Forgotten People*, 31–73.
10 'Compulsory Enrolment', paper prepared by the Chief Electoral Officer, R. C. Oldham, 6 October 1911, *Commonwealth Parliamentary Papers*, 1911, general vol. 2, no. 27. Senator George Pearce read large sections of this paper to the Senate, *CPD*, 6 October 1911, 11178.
11 *CPD*, 4 December 1911, 3633.
12 *CPD*, 5 December 1911, 3717.
13 Hobart *Mercury*, 14 October 1911, 4.
14 Weller & Lloyd, *Caucus Minutes*, 4 October 1911, 285.
15 *CPD*, 5 December 1911, 3709; 7 December 1911, 3931.
16 *CPD*, 7 December 1911, 4023.
17 *Commonwealth Year Book*, no. 16, 1923, 33790; Voting-age-population calculations based on population by age 1921, Australian Bureau of Statistics (ABS) cat. no. 3105.0.65.001, Australian Historical Population Statistics, Table 19, abs.gov.au/AUSSTATS/abs@.nsf/DetailsPage/3105.0.65.0012006?OpenDocument; accessed 31 January 2018.
18 Weller & Lloyd, *Caucus Minutes*, 17 October 1918, vol. 2, 71.

CHAPTER 10: VOTING ON SATURDAY

1   elections.org.nz/events/past-events/general-elections-1853-2014-dates-and-turnout; accessed 24 January 2017.
2   Report of Electoral Committee, 14 August 1901; Caucus Minutes, 27 July 1910, 14 October 1911, Weller & Lloyd, *Caucus Minutes*, 601, 263, 285.
3   New Zealand Government, 'Voter Turnout', stats.govt.nz/browse_for_stats/snapshots-of-nz/nz-social-indicators/Home/Trust%20and%20participation%20in%20government/voter-turnout.aspx; accessed 25 January 2018. New Zealand introduced compulsory registration in 1924: New Zealand Electoral Commission, Electoral Timeline.
4   Martin Wattenburg, 'Turnout Decline in the US and Other Advanced Industrialised Democracies', Centre for the Study of Democracy, UC Irvine Research Papers, cited by Hill, 'A Great Leveller', 136.
5   Rachel Gillett, 'You Can Take Time Off Work to Vote in 30 US States—But You're Out of Luck in the Rest', *Business Insider*, 6 November 2017.
6   Ella Saltmarshe, 'Too Busy to Vote? We're Asking Companies to Give Time Off on Election Day', *Guardian*, 7 June 2017; timetovote.co.uk.
7   *CPD*, Senate, 9 April 1902, 11472.
8   See Table 4 in Colin Hughes, 'Compulsory Voting', in C. Hughes (ed.), *Readings in Australian Government*, UQP, 1968, 232; James Fenton, *CPD*, 6 December 1911, 3938.
9   *CPD*, 6 December 1911, 3815 & 3812.
10 UWA, Australian Politics and Elections Database.
11 'How the People Voted', *Age*, 2 June 1913, 9.
12 Irving, 'Pulling the Trigger'.
13 *CPD*, 16 September 1913, 12289.
14 *CPD*, 16 September 1913, 12300.
15 *CPD*, 17 September 1913, 12734.
16 *SMH*, 3 October 1914, 14.

CHAPTER 11: QUEENSLAND MAKES IT COMPULSORY

1   RBA online pre-decimal inflation calculator.
2   Brisbane *Courier*, 4 November 1914, 7; Lindsay Smith, 'Compulsory Voting in Australia' in Lucy (ed.), *Pieces of Politics*, 232.

3   Brisbane *Courier*, 29 June 1915; UWA, Australian Politics and Elections Database.
4   Report of Federal Labor Conference, Brisbane *Courier*, 4 June 1915, 8; Caucus Minutes, 20 July 1917, Weller & Lloyd, 415.
5   Bennett, 'The Politics of Constitutional Amendment'.
6   Cited in Crisp, *The Australian Federal Labor Party*, 223.
7   *Argus*, 6 August 1915, 6.
8   Royal Commission on Electoral Matters and Administration, 16 July 1915. *Commonwealth Parliamentary Papers 1914–1917*, vol. 2, paper 180.
9   *CPD*, 8 September 1915, 6713–18.
10 Fitzhardinge, *The Little Digger*, vol. 2, 538.
11 Scott, *Australia during the War*, 352–53.
12 For the politics of the two conscription referenda, see Joan Beaumont, *Broken Nation*, 219–48 & 374–89; Hughes's quote, 226.

CHAPTER 12: THE FARMERS GET A PARTY

1   This history draws on Reid and Forrest, *Australia's Commonwealth Parliament*, 117–18; and on B. D. Graham, 'The Choice of Voting Methods in Federal Politics: 1902–1918'.
2   Bill introduced to House, 4 October 1918, *CPD*, 6669 ff; Tudor's reply, 24 October 1918, *CPD*, 7193 ff; see also Matthew Charlton's speech, 24 October 1918, *CPD*, 7202 ff.
3   Psephos: Adam Carr's Election Archive. psephos.adam-carr.net/countries/a/australia/1917/1917repsby.txt; accessed 27 December 2018.
4   *CPD*, Senate, 15 October 1919, 13308–47.
5   Hilary Rubenstein, 'Thomas Bakhap', *Biographical Dictionary of the Australian Senate*. John Uhr's article, 'Why We Chose Proportional Representation' alerted me to Bakhap's conviction.
6   UWA, Australian Politics and Elections Database.
7   In 1975 the Country Party changed its name to the National Country Party and in 1982 to its current name, the National Party of Australia, in a bid to broaden its electoral base by becoming a champion of conservative social values.

CHAPTER 13: COMPULSORY VOTING ACHIEVED

1   *Age*, 7 July 1916, 4; 3 August 1916, 6.
2   *Argus*, 1 December 1916, 6.
3   *Age*, 7 August 1917, 7.
4   *Age*, 19 December 1917, 8.
5   *CPD*, 7 November 1918, 7566–68.
6   *Age*, 7 August 1917, 7.
7   *Argus*, 21 October 1921, 7; *Age*, 7 September 1921, 10.
8   UWA, Australian Politics and Elections Database.
9   *Age*, 5 September 1921, 7.
10 These figures are from the second-reading speech of Senator Payne, who introduced the bill. They are slightly different from those given in the Australian Politics and Elections Database, but as these are the ones believed at the time they are the ones given here. *CPD*, 17 July 1924, 2180.
11 *Argus*, 16 July 1924, 19.
12 *Age*, 21 March 1923, 11.
13 Michael Roe, 'Payne, Herbert James Mockford (1866–1944)', *Biographical Dictionary of the Australian Senate*.
14 Antony Green, 'Review of the Robson Rotation', abc.net.au/news/2008-07-03/review-of-robson-rotation-in-tasmania/9389028; accessed 21 November 2018.

15 *Argus*, 18 July 1924, 11.
16 RBA online pre-decimal inflation calculator.
17 Payne's second-reading speech, *CPD*, 16 July 1924, 21802.
18 Anne Millar, 'Gardiner, Albert, (1867–1952)', *Biographical Dictionary of the Australian Senate*.
19 *CPD*, 17 July 1924, 2182.
20 *CPD*, 24 July 1924, 2446–52.
21 UWA, Australian Politics and Elections Database.
22 L. F. Crisp, 'Compulsory Voting in Australia', 88.
23 *Argus*, 1 December 1925, 11.
24 This is a based on the summaries of the states' electoral laws in Hughes & Graham, *Australian Government and Politics*.

CHAPTER 14: THE RISE OF MINOR PARTIES AND THE SENATE

1 Green, 'Explaining the Results'; and 'Preference Flows at the 2106 Election', abc.net.au/news/2016-09-15/preference-flows-at-the-2016-federal-election/9388826, accessed 14 August 2018.
2 Farrell & McAllister, *The Australian Electoral System*, 40–44; Uhr, 'Why We Chose Proportional Representation in the Senate'.
3 Tim Colebatch, 'Metre Long Ballot Paper Means Voters Will Need to Read the Fine Print', *SMH*, 18 August 2013.
4 AEC, ' Above the Line and Below the Line Voting', Senate Ballot Paper Study, 2016, aec.gov.au/About_AEC/research/files/sbps-atl-and-btl-voting.pdf; accessed 15 August 2018.
5 Marcus Priest, 'The Vote Broker Who Made the New Senate', *Australian Financial Review*, 10 September 2013.
6 aec.gov.au/Voting/How_to_Vote/Voting_Senate.htm; accessed 15 August 2018.

CHAPTER 15: LIBERALS PUSH BACK

1 Minchin, 'A Denial of Rights, A Detriment to Democracy', 244.
2 Minchin, Oral History Interview.
3 Minchin, 'A Denial of Rights, A Detriment to Democracy', 244–48.
4 See Hill, 'A Great Leveller', 133–35, and 'Compulsory Voting in Australia', 482–84.
5 Joint Standing Committee on Electoral Matters (JSCEM), Report of Inquiry into 1996 Federal Election.
6 Cited by Faulkner, *CPD*, 17 June 1997, 4372.
7 *CPD*, 17 June 1997, 4372–76.
8 *CPD*, 13 May 1997, 3379.
9 Green, 'The Constitutional Convention Election' in Warhurst & Mackerras (eds), *Constitutional Politics*, 29–40; AEC, 1997 Constitutional Convention Report and Statistics.
10 Evans, 'Compulsory Voting in Australia'.
11 'Howard Rejects Calls for Voluntary Voting', *SMH*, 5 October 2005.
12 This paragraph draws on Bennett, 'Compulsory Voting in Australian National Elections', 9–11.
13 Minchin, Oral History Interview.
14 *SMH*, 4 January 2014.
15 McAllister, *The Australian Voter*, 22–23.
16 JSCEM, Report of Inquiry into 1996 Federal Election, 25.
17 Horne & Magery, 'Electoral and Referendum Amendment'.
18 ABS Media Release 4517, 'Prisoners in Australia', 8 December 2017.
19 JSCEM, 'Report on the Conduct of the 2016 Election', Commonwealth Parliament, November 2018; Brent Holmes, 'Voter ID', Parliamentary Library, 4 August 2014; Graeme Orr, 'A Solution in Search of a Problem', *Inside Story*, 11 December 2018.

CHAPTER 16: AUSTRALIAN ELECTION DAYS

1. Malouf, 'A Spirit of Play', 111–12.
2. Charlwood, *All the Green Year*, ch. 16.
3. See Orr, *Ritual and Rhythm in Electoral Systems*, 113–15.
4. Hughes, 'The Bureaucratic Model', 119–20.
5. AEC, '2016 Federal Election: Key Facts and Figures', aec.gov.au/Elections/Federal_Elections/2016/key-facts.htm; accessed 24 September 2018.
6. 'Australian Word of the Year 2016', Oxford Australia Blog, blog.oup.com.au/2016/12/14/australian-word-of-the-year-2016; accessed 26 March 2018.
7. Simon White, 'Federal Election 2016: Bill Shorten Confounds by Eating Sausage Sizzle from Side', *SMH*, 2 July 2016.
8. Annabel Crabb, 'Not a Sausage', *SMH*, 9 April 1917.
9. sbs.com.au/news/the-feed/the-best-election-puns-from-cake-stalls-around-australia; accessed 26 March 2018.
10. Map, electionsausagesizzle.com.au/2016-federal-election-sausage-sizzle-map; accessed 22 October 2018.
11. Ley, *Commonwealth Electoral Procedures*, 29–30.
12. 'Voting from Abroad', International IDEA Handbook, Institute for Democracy and Electoral Assistance, 2007.
13. Tracey Gaw, Assistant Director, Elections Branch, personal communication.
14. Comment, reddit.com/r/australia/comments/4qttpe/happy_national_sausage_sizzle_day_please_share/d4vzbza; accessed 16 October 2018.
15. Howard, *The Menzies Era*, 7.
16. Griffen-Foley, *Party Games*, 78–80.
17. 'Albert Hall Centre for Votes Count', *Canberra Times*, 30 November 1963, 20; John Hay, television column, *Canberra Times*, 29 November 1966, 15.
18. JSCEM, Review of Certain Aspects of the Administration of the Australian Electoral Commission, ch. 4, 'Farewell to the National Tally Room', annualreport.aec.gov.au/2014/case-study/tally-room.html; accessed 26 March 2018.
19. JSCEM, Report on the Conduct of the 2007 Federal Election, ch. 7, aph.gov.au/Parliamentary_Business/Committees/Joint/Completed_Inquiries/em/elect07/report2; accessed 29 March 2018.
20. Brent, 'The Rise and Rise of the Early Voter', *Drum*, ABC News, 28 June 2016.
21. Jouljet, 'Election Day in Australia', 7 September 2013, jouljet.blogspot.com/2013/09/election-day-in-australia-do-we-even.html; accessed 9 November 2018.

CHAPTER 17: OF PLEBISCITES AND SURVEYS

1. ABS, Australian Marriage Law Postal Survey, National Results, abs.gov.au/ausstats/abs@.nsf/mf/1800.0; accessed 1 October 2018.
2. McKeown, 'Chronology of Same-Sex Marriage Bills'.
3. Opinion-poll results since 2004 are summarised in 'Public Opinion of Same-Sex Marriage in Australia', en.wikipedia.org/wiki/Public_opinion_of_same-sex_marriage_in_Australia; accessed 25 September 2018.
4. Australian Archives, 'Australia's National Anthem: Fact Sheet No. 251'; Curran & Ward, *The Unknown Nation*, ch. 5.
5. McKeown, 'Chronology of Same-Sex Marriage Bills'.
6. McKeown, 'Chronology of Same-Sex Marriage Bills'.
7. Australian Marriage Law Postal Survey, pandora.nla.gov.au/pan/164425/20170914-0705/marriagesurvey.abs.gov.au; accessed 25 September 2018.
8. Australian Marriage Law Postal Survey, pandora.nla.gov.au/pan/164425/20170914-0705/marriagesurvey.abs.gov.au; accessed 25 September 2018.

9. Melissa Cunningham, 'ABS Warns Australians Not to Post Same-Sex Marriage Forms Online', *SMH*, 14 September 2017.
10. Kate Mani, 'Second Pile of Same-Sex Marriage Surveys Found Dumped in Melbourne Laneway', *SMH*, 19 September 2017; SBS News, 'Concern Over People Boasting of Multiple Votes', 14 September 2017.
11. Louise Yaxley, 'Same-Sex Marriage Vote Irregular', ABC News, 10 August 2010.
12. 'Liberal Vice-President Hopeful "Silent Majority" Opposes Same-Sex Marriage', SBS News, 14 September 2017.
13. Channel Nine produced a video gallery of twenty-seven celebrities urging a Yes vote: 'Aussie Celebrities Throw Their Support Behind Same-Sex Marriage', celebrity.nine.com.au/2017/08/16/09/32/aussie-celebrities-throw-support-behind-same-sex-marriage#27.
14. 'Sydney Bars Are Becoming "Official" Voting Enrolment Venues for Marriage Equality', concreteplayground.com/sydney/news-2/sydney-bars-official-voting-enrolment-venues-promote-marriage-equality; Nick Bielby, 'King Street Hotel Helps Punters in Line-up Update Details ahead of Same-Sex Marriage Vote', *Newcastle Herald*, 18 August 2017.
15. AEC Media Release, 'Enrolment processing for the marriage survey completed', aec.gov.au/media/media-releases/2017/08-30.htm; accessed 1 October 2018. Michael Koziol, '"Extraordinary": 100,000 New Voters Join Electoral Roll as Last Minute Surge Buoys "Yes" Campaign', *SMH*, 25 August 2017.
16. 'ABS Chief Statistician David Kalisch Makes Nation Wait for SSM Answer', *Herald Sun*, 15 November 2017.
17. Michael Koziol, 'Same-Sex Marriage Survey', *SMH*, 13 November 2017, updated 15 November 2017.
18. Judith Ireland, 'Same-Sex Marriage Vote: Tony Abbott, Scott Morrison, Barnaby Joyce and Other MPs Who Didn't Vote "Yes" or "No"', *SMH*, 8 December 2017; 'Same-Sex Marriage Senate Decision', *SMH*, 29 November 2017.
19. Peter Dutton, 'The Same-Sex Marriage Postal Vote Worked But We Shouldn't Use It Again', *SMH*, 11 December 2017.

CHAPTER 18: WE ARE GOOD AT ELECTIONS

1. Bryce, *Modern Democracies*, vol. 2, 166.
2. Healy & Warden, 'Compulsory Voting', 8.
3. This argument is developed in Peter Brent's excellent PhD thesis, 'The Rise of the Electoral Officer'.
4. Orr, *The Law of Politics*, 207.
5. Cannon & McAllister, *Trends in Australian Political Opinion*, 18–29.
6. Michael Koziol, 'Distrustful Nation: Australians Lose Faith in Politics, Media and Business', *SMH*, 21 January 2017.
7. Howard, 'A Personal Response', 247–48.
8. See, for example, Paul Kelly, 'Main Parties Are Divided Because We Are Divided', *Australian*, 24 October 2018.
9. Ryan Goss, 'Votes for Corporations and Extra Votes for Property Owners: Why Local Council Elections Are Undemocratic', *Conversation*, 14 September 2017.
10. Joo-Cheong Tham, 'Australia's Growing Democracy Gap', *Inside Story*, 2 October 2018.

BIBLIOGRAPHY

Allan, Katherine. 'A Most Compelling Decision: Why Australia Forces its Citizens to Vote'. BA Honours Thesis, University of Melbourne, 2013.

Anderson, Carol. *One Person, No Vote: How Voter Suppression Is Destroying Our Democracy*. Bloomsbury, New York, 2018.

Atkinson, Jeffrey & David Roberts. '"Men of Colour": John Joseph and the Eureka Treason Trial'. *Journal of Australian Colonial History*, 10:1, 2008, 75–98.

Bannon, J. C. 'South Australia' in Helen Irving (ed.), *The Centenary Companion to Federation*.

Beaumont, Joan. *Broken Nation: Australians in the Great War*. Allen & Unwin, Sydney, 2013.

Beluch, James. *Replenish the Earth: The Settler Revolution and the Rise of the Anglo-World, 1783–1939*. Oxford University Press, Oxford, 2009.

Bennett, Scott. 'The Politics of Constitutional Amendment'. Research Paper no. 11, Australian Parliamentary Library, 2002–03.

Bennett, Scott. 'Compulsory Voting in Australian National Elections'. Research Brief, Australian Parliamentary Library, 31 October 2005.

Brent, Peter. 'The Rise of the Returning Officer: How Colonial Australia Developed Advanced Electoral Institutions'. PhD Thesis, Australian National University, 2008.

Brett, Judith. *Robert Menzies' Forgotten People*. Pan Macmillan, Melbourne, 1992.

Brett, Judith. *The Enigmatic Mr Deakin*. Text, Melbourne, 2017.

Bryce, James. *Modern Democracies*, vol. 2. Macmillan, New York, 1921.

Cameron, Sarah M. & Ian McAllister, 'Trends in Australian Political Opinion: Results from the Australian Election Study, 1987–2016'. School of Politics and International Relations, Australian National University, 2016.

Charlton, John. *The Chartists: The First National Workers' Movement*. Pluto Press, London, 1997.

Charlwood, Don. *All the Green Year*. Angus & Robertson, Sydney, 1965.

Chesterman, John & Brian Galligan. *Citizens without Rights: Aborigines and Australian Citizenship*. Cambridge University Press, Melbourne, 1997.

Collins, Hugh. 'Political Ideology in Australia: The Distinctiveness of a Benthamite Society'. *Daedalus*, 1:114, 1985, 147–69.

Crisp, L. F. *The Australian Federal Labor Party: 1901–1951*. Hale & Iremonger, Sydney, 1978.

Crisp, L. F. 'Compulsory Voting in Australia'. *Parliamentary Affairs*, IV:1, January 1950, 84–91.

Curran, James & Stuart Ward. *The Unknown Nation: Australia after Empire*. Melbourne University Press, Melbourne, 2010.

Davies, A. F. *Australian Democracy*. Longmans, Melbourne, 1958.

Davison, Graeme, John Hirst & Stuart Macintyre (eds). *Oxford Companion to Australian History*. Oxford University Press, Melbourne, 1998.

Dinwiddy, John. *Bentham*. Oxford University Press, Oxford, 1983.

Evans, Tim. 'Compulsory Voting in Australia'. Australian Electoral Commission, 16 January 2006.

Farrell, David & Ian McAllister. *The Australian Electoral System: Origins, Variations and Consequences*. UNSW Press, Sydney, 2006.

Faulkner, John & Stuart Macintyre (eds). *True Believers: The Story of the Federal Parliamentary Labor Party*, Allen & Unwin, Sydney, 2001.

Fitzhardinge, L. F. *The Little Digger: A Political Biography of William Morris Hughes*, vol. 2. Angus & Robertson, Sydney, 1979.

Garran, Robert. *Prosper the Commonwealth*. Angus & Robertson, Sydney, 1958.

Graham, B. D. 'The Choice of Voting Methods in Federal Politics, 1902–1918' in Colin Hughes (ed.), *Readings in Australian Government*. University of Queensland Press, Brisbane, 1968.

Green, Antony. 'The Constitutional Convention Election' in John Warhurst & Malcolm Mackerras (eds), *Constitutional Politics: The Republic Referendum and the Future*. University of Queensland Press, Brisbane, 2002.

Green, Antony. 'Explaining the Results' in Carol Johnson & John Wanna (eds), *Abbott's Gamble: The 2013 Australian Federal Election*. ANU Press, Canberra, 2015.

Griffen-Foley, Bridget. *Party Games: Australian Politicians and the Media from War to Dismissal*. Text, Melbourne, 2003.

Gow, Neil. 'The Introduction of Compulsory Voting in the Australian Commonwealth'. *Australian Journal of Political Science*, 6:2, 1971, 201–10.

Hancock, W. K. *Australia*. Ernest Benn, London, 1930.

Healy, Margaret & James Warden. 'Compulsory Voting'. Research Paper no. 24, Commonwealth Department of the Parliamentary Library, 1994–95.

Hill, Lisa. '"A Great Leveller": Compulsory Voting' in Marian Sawer (ed.), *Elections: Full, Free and Fair*.

Hill, Lisa. 'Compulsory Voting in Australia: A Basis for a Best Practice Regime'. *Federal Law Review*, 3:32, 2004, 479–98.

Hirst, John. 'Western Australia' in Graeme Davison et al, *Oxford Companion to Australian History*, 678–79.

Hirst, John. *Australia's Democracy: A Short History*. Allen & Unwin, Sydney, 2002.

Hirst, John. 'Making Voting Secret: Victoria's Introduction of a New Method of Voting that has Spread around the World'. Victorian Electoral Commission, Melbourne, 2006.

Hirst, John. *The Sentimental Nation: The Making of the Australian Commonwealth*. Oxford University Press, Melbourne, 2000.

Hirst, John. *The Strange Birth of Colonial Democracy: New South Wales, 1848–1884*. Allen & Unwin, Sydney, 1988.

Homeshaw, Judith. 'Inventing Hare-Clark: The Model Arithmetocracy' in Marian Sawer (ed.), *Elections: Full, Free and Fair*.

Horne, Nicholas & Kirsty Magery. 'Electoral and Referendum Amendment (Enrolment and Prisoner Voting) Bill 2010'. Bills Digest no. 71, Australian Parliamentary Library, 28 February 2011.

Howard, John. *The Menzies Era: The Years that Shaped Modern Australia*. HarperCollins, Sydney, 2014.

Howard, John. 'A Personal Response' in Tom Frame (ed.), *Back from the Brink: 1997–2001: The Howard Government*, vol. 2. UNSW Press, Sydney, 2018.

Hughes, C. & B. D. Graham. *A Handbook of Australian Government and Politics, 1890–1964*. Australian National University Press, Canberra, 1968.

Hughes, Colin. 'Compulsory Voting' in Colin Hughes (ed.), *Readings in Australian Government*. University of Queensland Press, Brisbane, 1968.

Hughes, Colin. 'The Bureaucratic Model: Australia'. *Journal of Behavioural and Social Sciences*, 37, 1992, 106–23.
Irving, Helen. 'Pulling the Trigger: The 1914 Double Dissolution Election and its Legacy'. *Papers on Parliament*, 63, 2015, 23–42.
Irving, Helen (ed.). *The Centenary Companion to Australian Federation*. Cambridge University Press, Melbourne, 1999.
John, Sarah & Donald A. DeBats. 'Australia's Adoption of Compulsory Voting: Revising the Narrative—Not Trailblazing, Uncontested or Democratic'. *Australian Journal of Politics and History*, 60:1, 2014, 1–27.
Joint Select Committee on Electoral Matters. Report of Inquiry into All Aspects of the 1996 Federal Election, June 1997.
Joint Select Committee on Electoral Matters. Review of Certain Aspects of the Administration of the Australian Electoral Commission, 18 September 2007.
Joint Select Committee on Electoral Matters. Report on the Conduct of the 2007 Federal Election and Matters Related Thereto, June 2009.
Ley, F. L. *Commonwealth Electoral Procedures and Other Information Relating to Elections and Electoral Matters*. Australian Government Publishing Service, Canberra, 1976.
McAllister, Ian. *The Australian Voter: Fifty Years of Change*. UNSW Press, Sydney, 2011.
McKenna, Mark. 'The Story of the Australian Ballot', in Marian Sawer (ed.), *Elections: Full, Free and Fair*.
McKeown, Dierdre. 'Chronology of Same-Sex Marriage Bills Introduced into the Federal Parliament: A Quick Guide'. Australian Parliamentary Library, 15 February 2018.
Mackerras, M. & I. McAllister. 'Compulsory Voting, Party Stability and Electoral Advantage in Australia'. *Electoral Studies*, 18, 1999, 217–33.
Magery, Susan. *Unbridling the Tongues of Women: A Biography of Catherine Helen Spence*. Hale & Iremonger, Sydney, 1985.
Malouf, David. 'A Spirit of Play: The Making of Australian Consciousness'. Boyer Lectures, ABC Books, Sydney, 1998.
Minchin, Nick. 'A Denial of Rights, A Detriment to Democracy'. *Parliamentarian*, 3:77, July 1996, 244–48.
Minchin, Nick. Oral-history interview by Susan Marsden, 19 October 2010. OH 955, State Library of South Australia.
Norberry, Jennifer & George Williams. 'Voters and the Franchise: The Federal Story'. Australian Parliamentary Library, Research Paper no. 17, 2001–02.
Orr, Graeme, Bryan Mercurio & George Williams (eds). *Realising Democracy: Electoral Law in Australia*. Federation Press, Sydney, 2003.
Orr, Graeme & George Williams. 'The People's Choice: The Prisoner Franchise and the Constitutional Protection of Voting Rights in Australia'. *Election Law Journal*, 8:12, 2007.
Orr, Graeme. *The Law of Politics: Elections, Parties and Money in Australia*. Federation Press, Sydney, 2010.
Orr, Graeme. *Ritual and Rhythm in Electoral Systems: A Comparative Legal Account*. Routledge, Oxford, 2016.
Overacker, Louise. *The Australian Party System*. Yale University Press, New Haven, 1952.
Reid, G. S. & Martyn Forrest. *Australia's Commonwealth Parliament, 1901–1908: Ten Perspectives*. Melbourne University Press, Melbourne, 1989.

Reynolds, Henry. *This Whispering in Our Hearts*. Allen & Unwin, Sydney, 1998.
Richardson, Henry Handel. *The Fortunes of Richard Mahony*. Australian Classics edition, Angus & Robertson, Sydney, 1983.
Roberts, Tony. 'The Brutal Truth: What Happened in the Gulf Country'. *Monthly*, November 2007.
Rowse, Tim. *Indigenous and Other Australians Since 1901*. UNSW Press, Sydney, 2017.
Rydon, Joan. 'Electoral Methods' in Marian Simms (ed.), *1901: The Forgotten Election*.
Sawer, Geoffrey. *Australian Politics and Law, 1901–1929*. Melbourne University Press, Melbourne, 1956.
Sawer, Marian (ed.). *Elections: Full, Free and Fair*. Federation Press, Sydney, 2001.
Sawer, Marian. 'Enrolling the People' in Graeme Orr et al (eds), *Realising Democracy: Electoral Law in Australia*.
Sawer, Marian & Sarah Miskin (eds). 'Representation and Institutional Change: Fifty Years of Proportional Representation in the Senate'. *Papers on Parliament*, 34, December 1999.
Scott, Ernest. *A Short History of Australia*. 8th edition, Oxford University Press, Melbourne, 1950.
Scott, Ernest. *The Official History of Australia in the War of 1914–18: Australia during the War*, vol. 9. Angus & Robertson, Sydney, 1936.
Serle, Geoffrey. *The Golden Age: A History of the Colony of Victoria 1851–1861*. Melbourne University Press, Melbourne, 1977.
Simms, Marian (ed.). *1901: The Forgotten Election*. University of Queensland Press, Brisbane, 2001.
Smith, Lindsay. 'Compulsory Voting in Australia' in Richard Lucy (ed.), *Pieces of Politics*. Macmillan, Melbourne, 1983.
Spence, Catherine Helen. 'A Plea for Pure Democracy: Mr Hare's Reform Bill Applied to South Australia'. Rigby, South Australia, 1861.
Spence, Catherine Helen. *An Autobiography*. W. K. Thomas, Adelaide, 1910.
Stretton, Pat & Christine Finnimore. 'Black Fellow Citizens: Aborigines and the Commonwealth Franchise'. *Australian Historical Studies*, 25:101, 1993, 522–23.
Taylor, Greg. 'The Early Life of Mr Justice Boothby'. *Adelaide Law Review*, 34, 2013, 167–200.
Thompson, M. M. H. *The First Election: The New South Wales Legislative Council Election of 1843*. Max Thompson, Goulburn, 1993.
Trollope, Anthony. *An Autobiography*. Oxford University Press World Classics edition, Oxford, 1980.
Uhr, John. 'Rules for Representation: Parliament and the Design of the Australian Electoral System' in G. Lindell & R. Bennett (eds), *Parliament: The Vision in Hindsight*. Federation Press, Sydney, 2001.
Uhr, John. 'Why We Chose Proportional Representation' in Marion Sawer & Sarah Miskin (eds), 'Representation and Institutional Change: Fifty Years of Proportional Representation in the Senate'.
Weller, Patrick & Beverley Lloyd. *Caucus Minutes, 1901–1917: Minutes of the Meetings of the Federal Parliamentary Labor Party*, vol. 1. Melbourne University Press, Melbourne, 1975.
Wright, Clare. *You Daughters of Freedom: The Australians Who Won the Vote and Inspired the World*. Text, Melbourne, 2018.

LIST OF ILLUSTRATIONS

1. 'Facts about the Ballot': reproduced in Anthony Trollope, *An Autobiography*, Oxford University Press, 1950.

2. Catherine Helen Spence: State Library of South Australia, B46492.
3. Mary Lee: State Library of South Australia, B70647.
4. Henry Chapman: in Redmond Barry's bound volume of photos, *Fasti Victorienses*, vol. 27, p. 95. Batchelder & O'Neill, Melbourne. State Library of Victoria.
5. William Boothby: State Library of South Australia, B8073.

6. Cover of *Australian Woman's Sphere*, vol. 1, no. 2, October 1900: State Library of Victoria.
7. 'How to Vote on Federation Day': State Library of South Australia.

8. Brisbane, 1907: State Library of Queensland.
9. R. C. Oldham: Pen and ink drawing by Hal Gye, *Bulletin*, 5 February 1920. National Library of Australia.
10. Herbert Payne: T. Humphrey & Co., Melbourne. National Library of Australia.
11. Richard O'Connor: Swiss Studios, Melbourne. National Library of Australia.

12. Etajima, 1946: *Argus* Newspaper Collection of Photographs, State Library of Victoria.
13. ACT, 1960s: National Archives of Australia, A1500 K21453.

14. Sydney Town Hall, 1966: Photograph by John Tanner. National Archives of Australia, A1200 L58979.
15. *Don's Party*: Cover photograph by Jeff Busby. Courtesy of Currency Press.
16. National Tally Room, 1969: National Archives of Australia, A1200 L39309.

17. Bondi, 1966: Photograph by John Tanner. National Archives of Australia, A1200 L58975.
18. Darwin, 1960s: National Archives of Australia, A1200 L84788.
19. Davis, 2016: Photograph by Alison Dean. Australian Antarctic Division.

20. Footscray City Primary School, 2018: Victorian Electoral Commission.
21 & 22. Merri Creek Primary School, 2018: Photographs by David Trembath.
23. Southbank, 2018: Photograph by Judith Brett.

ALSO AVAILABLE FROM TEXT

JUDITH BRETT

THE ENIGMATIC MR DEAKIN

'Extraordinary…Few Australian prime ministers can match the allure of Deakin.' **Mark McKenna**

'Revealing and insightful.' **Paul Kelly**

'Utterly compelling.' **Clare Wright**

'A biography of immense power.' **David Marr**

TEXTPUBLISHING.COM.AU